THERE AND BACK
AGAIN... ALMOST

A Pennine Way walk – 400 miles
up and down the spine of England,
wild camping (nearly) all the way

Will Cove

DEDICATION

To my long-suffering family, Jo, Mia and Florence,
for letting me go and allowing me to come back.

THANKS

Many thanks to Dawn Leggott, a good friend, who
proofread this account, turning my ramblings into a
coherent script.

CONTENTS

THE ROUTE

I wasn't going to write up this walk, so I was a little surprised to find myself typing at my laptop. I didn't feel that it would be a particularly epic adventure. Being the original and oldest national trail in the UK, it is well trodden with many resupply points along the route. The trail doesn't wander too far into remote territory. Much of the path is covered in hefty flagstones. There are cafes, pubs and B&Bs in abundance. At over 250 miles it is a long walk, but I didn't think it would be anything to write home about. I changed my mind about documenting my Pennine Way stroll around day seven of the walk. Walking during the Covid-19 pandemic, just coming out of the third UK lockdown, meant B&Bs, pubs and campsites were closed to overnight stays. This necessitated wild camping all the way, which much reduced human interaction. I'd forgotten how cathartic I find long periods of solitude. It was the desire to capture my state of mind, and perhaps because I found it therapeutic, that I started writing about my experience as I walked, repurposing my used map tiles as notepaper, as I had done on my previous endeavours.

IN THE BEGINNING

Yes, I had done a few long distance walks before. I cut my teeth on Wainwright's coast to coast. This was followed by a baptism of fire, or more accurately an ordeal by ice, on the Southern Upland Way and then rounded off with a personal spiritual odyssey on the Cape Wrath Trail – 247 miles through the West Highland wilderness. With those three walks I thought I'd sated my long distance walking desires and proved anything I had to prove to myself. Definitively and done. I find that, apparently, I haven't.

It was at the end of walking the Cape Wrath Trail that I'd posted a few photos on Facebook and a friend had asked, "What's next?" (thanks Dawn). I hadn't really thought much about the next challenge, but from the Cape Wrath lighthouse, the most northwesterly point of mainland Britain, I reflected that as the CWT was about as far as I could get from my home, then maybe I should find something a little more local next time. I live on the northern edge of the Peak District, under an hour's drive from Edale, the starting point for the Pennine Way. The Peak District was my back yard playground. I'd flown above it on paragliders and walked across it extensively for more than two decades. But whilst I had walked between Edale and the M62 a handful of times, I hadn't given any thought to meandering further north.

In August 2020, arriving home from a second year of exploring Europe (and a little further) with the family in our camper van, I pondered upon a challenge to set myself and naturally concluded that the Pennine Way should be it. Having completed the Cape Wrath Trail, hailed as the toughest long distance walk that nobody had ever heard of, I was confident to the point of being blasé about walking the Pennine Way.

FAIL TO PLAN, PLAN TO FAIL!

I ventured out on a few weekend sojourns to reacquaint myself with the skills and equipment required for long distance walking. My first foray found me hopelessly lost for several hours, stumbling through the heather on Bleaklow, having somehow forgotten that I needed to orientate my phone north when using the ViewRanger maps. One jaunt resulted in a sleepless night and my tent in tatters on Kinder after I miscalculated the wind high up. Not a cheap lesson at £140 for a new tent pole and flysheet repairs. I abandoned another weekend walk, again after underestimating the weather. Finding myself freezing and with minimal visibility in a blizzard, I retreated from Bleaklow to the nearest road. I phoned my wife and pleaded to be rescued.

During one of my long distance walking revision exercises I bumped into a dad and son crossing the Snake Pass road. They both had large packs and walking poles. Large packs and poles are the hallmark of multi-day walkers. The dad eagerly explained that they were walking the Pennine Way. He'd been planning it for years and claimed it was the "Daddy of National Trails". I almost retorted that if the Pennine Way was the "Daddy of National Trails" then my last walk, the CWT, was "The

Godfather". I bit my tongue, kept schtum and berated myself for such churlish thoughts. It was not the time for a bragging competition. I told them of a good wild camp spot that I knew of north of Crowden and wished them well with an abridged version of the Irish blessing, "May the wind always be on your back and may the sun warm your face."

Duly humbled by some of my weekend fails, it dawned on me that it would be wise to show the Pennine Way a bit of respect. I could have invested in one of the readily available guidebooks, but that wasn't my modus operandi. For previous walks I had used the dark, cold, winter months preceding departure to scour the internet for information about facilities and crux points along the route. I set about reading blogs and watching YouTube videos, gathering intelligence. I painstakingly stitched together in Photoshop screen grabs from ViewRanger OS 1:125k overlay to produce a custom-made strip map. I added all the notes I'd gleaned, along with supermarket and post office locations and opening times. I also added locations of pubs, B&Bs and campsites. Alas, this accommodation information was obsolete, as Covid restrictions meant that they remained closed. I liked the idea of wild camping and that was how I had spent many nights on the walks I had already completed. However, it also felt committing to not have the backup option of a warm cosy night at a pub or B&B. On previous walks, campsites, hostels, pubs and bothies had proven essential safe havens to escape foul weather, dry out and restore tattered morale. Without the safety net, I was at the mercy of whatever elements came my way. I viewed the entire route with Google's satellite overlay to pinpoint possible wild camping locations. I split the final Photoshop document up into 28cm-square pages, with each page the size of my Ortlieb map case. The end result was 44 map tiles. My guide from Edale to Kirk Yetholm.

My research showed I would hit a Co-op or Spar at least once every two days, so I wasn't too concerned about resupplying food. However, I supplemented my nutritional needs with three food parcels for me to pick up along the route. I sent them for the attention of "Will Cove, Post Restante" to the post offices at Hawes, Alston and Bellingham. I hadn't used the post office's Post Restante service since backpacking around South East Asia in the 1990s. In a time before email and mobile phones, it was the only way of receiving mail from home. This time the parcels' main content was my pre-prepared breakfast of choice: a ziplock bag of Readybrek, powdered milk, raisins and a generous dollop of golden syrup. Just add boiling water for a quick and easy no mess warming start to the day.

With my food sorted I turned my attention to my clothes. Travelling light dictated that I take the minimal amount. I had one set of day clothes and one set of night clothes. I was quite happy not washing my thermal pyjamas for two weeks, as all I was doing was sleeping in them. From toes to head my day clothes were: merino wool mid-weight socks, which can easily stand over a week of heavy sweaty use without beginning to whiff; my trousers, which could live with getting grubby; and a merino wool base layer which, again, can happily cope with neglect. I am amazed at the anti-bacterial power of merino wool. My fleece top was lightly used. That just left my boxer shorts...

I was quite happy wild camping along the route with minimal washing, but the thought of wearing the same underwear for two weeks was a little daunting even for me. I admit my threshold for dirt and grime is pretty high, but not having clean boxer shorts for so long was a leap too far. I wasn't prepared to carry all the underwear needed from the start. That went against the travelling light grain. I hatched a plan to take just one pair of boxer shorts and throw them away when I picked up my resupply parcel, which included a fresh set of briefs. Genius idea! Now wait, before you accuse me of wanton profligacy for throwing away my underwear with wild abandonment, let me let you into a secret. I, and I suspect I'm like most men, have several pairs of boxer shorts lurking at the back of my smalls drawer which should have been retired and repurposed as dusters a long time ago. They are probably now at the stage where they couldn't decently be used as dusters and are even beyond use as oil rags. Instead of throwing these suspect garments into landfill I thought I'd give them one last hurrah. A Viking burial so to speak. Alas, in the end I was unable to burn them due to fire risk, although incineration would have undoubtedly been the most hygienic way to dispose of them.

I now had my kit honed, map and route information dialled in, food and clothes sorted. I just needed to set off.

KIT LIST

GEAR

Terra Nova Laser Competition 1, tent pegs (6x MSR Mini Groundhogs, 6x titanium nails), cord

Thermarest Neo Air 3/4 sleeping mat, Sea to Summit Spark II sleeping bag, Alpkit Cloud Cover quilt

Soto Wind Master Stove, gas canister, pan, spork, lighter, small penknife, plastic mug, stove wind shield

Petal Tikkina headlight

Osprey Exos 38-litre backpack

Black Diamond Trail Back trekking poles

Water purification bottle, Sawyer Mini water filter, Platypus water bladder

Sunglasses, reading glasses

Plasters, ibuprofen & paracetamol tablets, needle, thread, scissors, scalpel blades, tape, dressings, Savlon, toilet paper, silver emergency blanket, tick remover tool, key-ring LED torch

Compact mirror, disposable razor, soap, toothbrush, toothpaste, towel (square foot)

Cash, debit card

Phone, charging cable, Alpkit solar panel

Ortlieb map case & self-made 1:25k map in ziplock bag, compass x2

Dry bags x3, heavy duty pee Bag

Foam seat pad

CLOTHES DAY

Sealskinz socks x 1, Merino socks x 1, thin socks x 1, boxer shorts x 2

Shorts x 1, T-shirt x 1, Merino top x 1, fleece top x 1, Rab trousers x 1

Montane Alpine Pro Gore-Tex jacket, Montane Gore-Tex trousers, Rab gaiters

Warm hat, sun hat, Outdoor Research Surge Sensor inner gloves, Montane Prism outer gloves

Berghaus Supalite II GTX walking boots

Neoprene shoes (for river crossings)

CLOTHES NIGHT

Subzero thermal top, Subzero thermal leggings, Heat Holder socks, Rab Zero G down jacket

READY... STEADY...

My original plan was to be dropped off at Kirk Yetholm by my family, officially the end of the Pennine Way, and walk south. I had originally thought to start a week before Easter, which was the start of my children's Easter holidays. I had thought I'd get to Black Hill and veer east and walk home, just four hours away. I'd done the Edale to Black Hill section both ways several times already so wasn't concerned about missing that bit. Well, that was the original plan, but then reality intervened.

As the third lockdown dragged on, I was beginning to wonder if I'd be walking the Pennine Way before summer. Fortunately the rules to stay local in England were lifted just after the Easter weekend; however, it was still illegal to travel to Scotland. The possibility of my family camping at Kirk Yetholm for the weekend and seeing me off was no longer an option. I decided that flexibility is the key to any successful plan and that I'd start from Edale and walk north. Hopefully by the time I arrived at the Scottish border, several weeks later, I would be allowed in and my family could meet me there. As I was now doing the trail in the traditional direction, south to north, and no longer walking home, it felt right to start at Edale, the official departure point.

My new plan was to walk north and hopefully be met by my family at the end, where they'd whisk me back home.

GO!
DAY 1

Edale to Kinder Downfall
Weather: Clear cool evening
5 miles
1600ft ascent

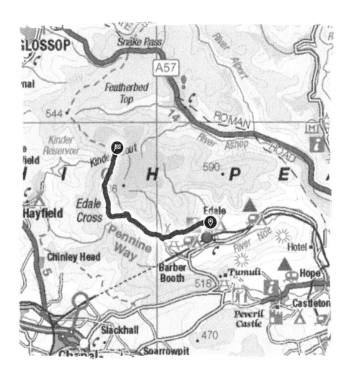

From previous experience I had learned the hard and painful way that putting in a big first day with a heavy pack can lead to problems, especially for my knees. After a couple of miles along the Edale valley floor, the Pennine Way climbs sharply up Jacob's Ladder, around Kinder Scout, down across Snake Pass, on over Bleaklow, down to Torside Reservoir and then past Crowden. It's a good 20 miles to the first wild camp spot just south of Black Hill. Twenty miles on the first day would probably equal pain and possibly failure. I decided to break myself in gently. It also tied in with my wife's work schedule.

So it was that on Friday 9th April 2021 at 4pm my wife, kids and I bundled into the family hatchback and set off across Strines Moor to Edale. It's a journey I have made hundreds, if not thousands, of times, but this time my senses were heightened with anticipation and the world felt sharpened and crystal clear. It was a lovely afternoon. The forecast was for the odd snow shower over the weekend but nothing serious. The outlook was for dry, cool, sunny weather. Perfect weather for walking.

Arriving at Edale I noticed, for the first time, that Edale was twinned with Kirk Yetholm. How had I missed this small but significant detail before? We tried to find a free place to park in the village but were thwarted by double yellow lines, so we returned to the large pay and display car park. I'm not so stingy that I wasn't prepared to pay a couple of quid, but I didn't have any change. Walking to the payment meter I met a traffic warden and asked if it was possible to pay by card. He replied that it wasn't. My heart sank. He then handed me an all-day parking ticket that someone had thoughtfully stuck on the meter before they had departed. Result!

We left the traffic warden writing out parking fines for one unfortunate Porsche owner and one unlucky Range Rover owner, both of whom had neglected to purchase parking tickets. He wondered aloud why the drivers couldn't stump up the two pound parking fee when they had sufficient funds for such expensive vehicles.

I wasn't exactly sure where the start to the Pennine Way was. We walked to the Old Nags Head and found a gate with a rather rough map outlining the route between Edale and Kirk Yetholm. I took a quick photo to use as reference just in case I happened to lose my maps. My family walked with me a mile out of Edale and we said goodbye at the foot of Broadlee Bank. I've always been hopeless at goodbyes. I was primed and ready to go. I gave each of them a hug and then moseyed on. Four hundred metres later, at the point where I was to lose line of sight, I turned to wave a final goodbye. They waved back. I took a deep breath, cut the cord and strode on.

I began climbing Jacob's Ladder. It is a steep climb but doesn't go on too long. I had danced up the uneven rocky steps before. This time I purposely measured my pace. Speed was not the short-term goal. I tried to keep my eye on the long game. Slow and easy. Gently, gently. Easing myself in. Only 250 miles to go.

At 6pm the few people I passed were heading down to the valley after a good day's adventure and on their way home; however, just beyond the top of Jacob's Ladder I briefly tailed a backpack clad walker and dog who'd walked up from Hadfield. They peeled off route and meandered down to Mermaid's Pool to camp for the night. I followed the Pennine Way around the Kinder plateau perimeter stopping at Kinder Downfall to pick up water. I'd thought about walking further, but at 7pm and the wind being on the gentle side of doable, I made the call to camp high. I could see a couple of tents down below and another not far from me on the plateau. I was surprised at just how popular Kinder was, and hoped they were all responsible wild campers.

I scouted the peat cloughs to find a sheltered hidden corner. Once my tent was pitched, bed made and supper slurped, I retook the high ground to witness my first sunset on my first day of the Pennine Way. With my plastic camping mug charged with Metaxa (my brandy of choice), I 'cheersed' the day and drank to happy trails.

Sunset on Kinder.

DAY 2

Kinder Downfall to Swellands Reservoir
Weather: Cold, snowy day
21.5 miles
3500ft ascent

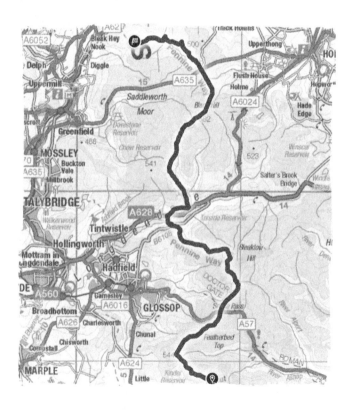

It was a cold night. Temperatures were sub-zero. I generally feel the cold and was very happy with a last-minute purchase I had made – a down quilt that had arrived just in time on the morning of the day of my departure. The quilt supplemented my two-season down sleeping bag and a down jacket. I lay up on the lofty chilled Kinder plateau, grateful to the geese that had sacrificed their feathers for the sake of my warmth. Whilst I had been assured by various outdoor clothing/equipment manufacturers that all the down from my insulating layers had been responsibly sourced, I felt a certain mindful obligation to acknowledge the deceased feathered fowl for their unwitting gift. I did not take their sacrifice lightly. Somewhere in my mind I hoped that their spirits soared. I suspect the deceased birds would have preferred to have continued soaring with the use of their own feathers. My conscience will be left to forever tussle with the dichotomy of ethics verse function. Judge me as you will.

Awake before the sunrise, after my tea and Readybrek breakfast taken snug within my sleeping bag, I braced myself for the chilly day. I snapped a couple of photos of the icy patterns that had formed on the tent flysheet. A few solitary snowflakes fluttered from the low cloud as I scraped ice off my tent and packed up. Yomping down from the Kinder plateau across to Snake Pass with a few hardy sheep my only companions, the snowfall became more insistent. The wintry conditions didn't concern me too much. As long as I kept moving I was warm and, due to my familiarity with this part of the trail, finding my way was easy. All I had to do was to follow the long line of flagstones across Featherbed Moss. After a couple of hours and atop Bleaklow, I took advantage of a brief pause in the snow showers to take a standing up break and snaffle some nuts and a Twix. I didn't stop for long. The imperative was to keep moving to stay warm. The gentle snowfall became heavy, with the snow beginning to settle deeper on the ground. Fortunately the wind was light, which made the walking peaceful and muffled through the winter wonderland.

On the long slope down to Torside Reservoir I passed a young bloke heading south with walking poles and a heavy pack, so guessed he was possibly another wayfarer. However, I soon dismissed the idea, as he appeared far too clean and fresh. He was more likely just out for the weekend. Crossing the reservoir dam head I passed another fellow, also with a large pack and poles. This chap had a weathered complexion and sported the beginnings of a healthy beard. Definitely a fellow wayfarer, but unfortunately the weather conditions didn't encourage stopping for a chat, so we merely exchanged nods as we passed one another.

North of Crowden I did the best I could to find enough shelter from the falling snow at Oaken Clough to take a break for a swift pot noodle pit stop. I slurped the noodles with as little dallying as I could muster before moving on above Laddow Rocks. Where the way drops down to meet Crowden Brook is an ideal wild camp spot, just big enough for a tent. On previous jaunts between Crowden and Black Hill I hadn't managed to camp there, but on this occasion I found a tent-shaped grass patch in the otherwise snow-covered terrain – evidence that someone else had recently spent the night there.

Walking up Black Hill, which was temporarily White

Hill, the snowfall became more intermittent. I could clearly see the Emley Moor mast to the east. A Flash Gordon-esque concrete structure some 95 feet higher than the Eiffel Tower, the mast is a telecommunications and broadcasting facility, which was built in 1964 and is now a Grade II listed building. I waved a hello to my family snug in our house not far from the foot of the mast. Looking north, the countryside was more green than white and I hoped I was leaving the snow behind.

By the time I passed the Wessenden reservoirs it was late afternoon and I was feeling weary. The wind was light enough to allow camping high and I began to scope out potential camp spots. I had walked further than I wished by the time I reached Swellands and Black Moss reservoirs and so deemed the location a perfect place to pitch the tent. Black Moss felt sufficiently far from roads and houses for me not to be troubled by anyone. The reservoirs supplied me with ample water for my needs. It wasn't long before I had my tent up and I was ensconced in my sleeping bag and quilt with chorizo and macaroni cheese bubbling on the stove. I screwed up the first four now-used and obsolete map tiles and pushed them to the bottom of my boots. I hoped they might absorb moisture and mitigate some of the dampness from the day's earlier slushy snowy walking. Around 9pm, with the last of the day's light fading, I soon fell sleep.

A hardy sheep below Kinder.

Black Hill was temporarily white hill.

DAY 3

Swellands Reservoir to May's
Weather: Cold, clear morning and hailstorms in the afternoon
18 miles
2350ft ascent

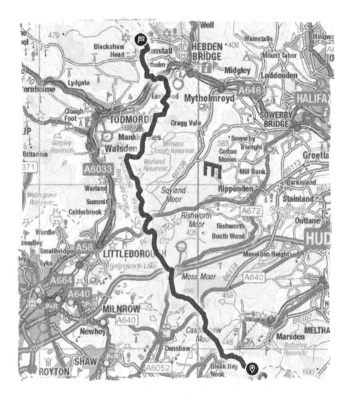

Drifting from sleep to consciousness I became aware of the tent flysheet gently resting on my nose. In the space between dreaming and rousing I briefly felt disorientated. Had I somehow become bigger in the night like Alice in Wonderland? Maybe by taking the "Drink Me" potion, but instead of shrinking I had grown? Had I, like Gulliver, been transported to Lilliput and the world around me had become miniaturised? Waking properly, I extracted my hand from my sleeping bag and pushed the nylon fabric. It resisted gently, heavy on my hand. It slowly dawned on me that my tent was covered in a blanket of snow. I batted the flysheet, knocking the snow off the tent, and restored my living space to its usual size. Unzipping the door and peering out I was met by a beautiful winter scene of searingly clear, intense, pale blue sky and a blinding white land. It appeared that the people at the Met Office had underestimated the "light snow showers". It was the first time I had camped in snow with this tent and was quietly impressed at how well my flimsy lightweight shelter had coped with the conditions.

Recovering my gas canister from the bottom of my bed, I screwed in the stove and boiled up water for tea and breakfast. I had learned the hard way that gas doesn't work well in freezing conditions. The gas canister always spent the night with me at the end of my sleeping bag.

My least favourite part of the day was getting dressed. Once I had relinquished the warmth of my sleeping bag and shed my cosy night attire, I raced to pull on my day clothes, Gore-Tex shell, over trousers and down jacket. The task of packing my bedding away and battling to reinstall it in my backpack usually restored my warmth.

I'd then don my boots and gaiters before venturing out to break camp.

The morning walking was ethereal through the white wonderland. I wondered if I might suffer from snow blindness as all was bright white. I was annoyed that I had neglected to bring my sunglasses, as my eyes were beginning to sting. I did my best to focus on a set of muddy boot prints that I was following as a tactic to reduce the dazzling glare. It was very different to the last time I had walked across Standedge a few months earlier on a family weekend lockdown walk. Then it had been dressed in its more usual attire of sodden muted greens and yellows. I was reminded how transformative a blanket of snow can be to a landscape, converting the potentially foreboding countryside into a surreal enchanted scene.

Just before the M62 I stumbled upon a van selling food in a lay-by. I've always felt this van was some kind of mythical phantom dining experience that materialises once every blue moon when the planets are aligned and the god of snot has sneezed in the west. I had read accounts of this culinary destination but alas, until now, had found it absent. Not wanting to faff about in case it disappeared before my eyes, I swiftly relieved the mobile chef of a fine bacon and egg butty before passing through more snow-covered vistas and reservoirs.

It was Sunday and many families were out taking advantage of the late seasonal snowfall. Sledging, snowman building and general snowy shenanigans abounded all around. Stopping for an afternoon brew and channelling my inner Shackleton of the Antarctic spirit, I melted snow for the water for my tea. I noted that the current climate was akin to fridge temperature, allowing for perfectly preserved milk without the need for me to carry a fridge. A definite benefit in the fresh milk to fridge hauling weight ratio.

By mid-afternoon the clouds had built up and were popping. Long distance walking attunes me to the atmospheric conditions. Spending the entire day outside with nothing better to do than a bit of map reading, looking where to put my feet and observing the sky from morning till dusk, I become hyper aware of the weather. To say it looked threatening was an understatement. An ill-equipped couple passed me inquiring about the most direct route back to civilisation. I pointed them to a path down to Mankinholes and on to Todmorden. A hail shower finally caught up with me as I arrived at Stoodley Pike. I was somewhat surprised that the weather had taken so long to find me. To paraphrase Batfink, my Gore-Tex shell was like a shield of steel against the elements.

The monument marked another lockdown weekend family walk we had done a couple of months earlier and I forwent the opportunity to climb the dingy internal staircase to see the same view as the one from outside the structure. I headed down into the Hebden Bridge valley where I became separated from the Pennine Way due to sparse signposting and a tangle of national trails. My map told me that the only way is up (thanks, Yazz[1]). It was a steep climb back up onto the tops. This was followed by a temporary down across Jack Bridge then up to Colden. I arrived at May's "Aladdin's Cave" village farm shop (legendary on the Pennine Way) and quaffed a steak pie.

1. 1988 UK number one single "The Only Way Is Up" by Yazz and the Plastic Population.

It was just past 4pm but I was ready to stop. I had read that May lets wayfarers camp for free, but due to Covid guidelines she wasn't officially allowed to host walkers until the following day when restrictions were due to ease. The young girl who served me in the shop suggested I wild camp back at Jack Bridge, which I had just passed. I asked her if she could fill up my water bladder and she obligingly took it inside the farm house to fill it. When she returned, she reported that "the boss" said that I was OK to stay. Clearly Covid guidelines are flexible in these parts.

I camped in a field full of lambs just behind the shop and managed to get my tent up a moment before another graupel shower hit. I dived inside my nylon sanctuary, pulling on my sleeping bag and quilt to snuggle up warm. It was another cold night.

A frosty sunrise.

This much snow wasn't forecast!

Which way?

Winter wonderland.

Stormy clouds above Stoodley Pike.

DAY 4

May's to Pinhaw Hilltop
Weather: Sunny but chilly
18.5 miles
2900ft ascent

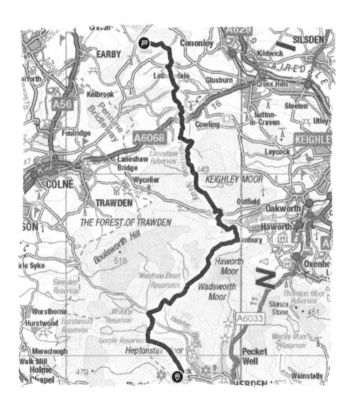

I was up and off at my now usual early hour but not before taking advantage of May's outside toilet, thus forgoing the necessity to dig a hole.

Over Heptonstall Moor the scenery was beginning to feel a little wilder. With another clear sunny day I enjoyed a morning brew by Walshaw Dean reservoirs. The day was cool enough for me to pull on my down jacket when I stopped in order to preserve the warmth I had built up whilst walking. It was a habit I was to deploy throughout my walk. I passed Top Withins, the inspiration for Brontë's Wuthering Heights, which was looking suitably wuthering with a sprinkling of snow. I noticed that the waymarker posts also had Japanese script pointing the Brontë Way. This was testament to the Brontë sisters' international appeal.

I bumped into a chap litter picking and we stopped for a chat. He had walked the Pennine Way in 1979, back in the day before lightweight equipment, mobile phones and handheld GPS devices. And before the peat bogs between Kinder and the Snake Pass had been flagged with paving stones. He explained he had stashed supplies along the Way in advance and that the ethos when confronted with treacherous quagmires was to embrace the bog as part of the adventure. "A different age," I thought to myself.

Along with my quilt, another last-minute addition to my kit had been a solar panel. It had arrived on the morning of departure which left me no time to test how well it worked. At 300 grammes it was 100 grammes lighter than my power bank. At a difference of only 100 grammes I was aware that I was entering "geek" level territory on the lightweight backpacking front. I was also aware that I was exactly the type of person who cuts the labels off my clothing and equipment to save weight. I even cut my toothbrush in half. But that was more about me not liking labels and long toothbrush handles than anything to do with the fraction of grammes that I shaved from my backpack load. More relevant was the solar panel's potentially longer-term solution to phone charging. I knew I was taking a bit of a gamble swapping out the power bank for the untested solar panel. I didn't know how effective it would be or how fragile it was.

Apart from the first two wintry days of the walk I had been fortunate to have clear skies and sunshine most of the day. With a couple of small carabiners attaching the solar panel to the top of my pack and a lead running to my phone in my pocket I usually found that by midday my phone was fully charged after the previous evening's and a morning's use. Maybe 20% to 30% charge of my phone. This was brilliant. It meant that I could move from ultra energy saving mode to keeping my phone turned on all the time, albeit in airplane mode. This facilitated plentiful photos and easy navigation checks.

The way took me across farmland and through hamlets. All very pleasant, but the hamlets were not large enough to offer shops or cafes and the farmland was not wild enough to instill adventure.

My wife messaged me and asked if I was enjoying myself. I replied answering obliquely that it was a long, long, long walk. I had walked over 60 miles with just under 200 miles to go. Inwardly I wondered if I was enjoying myself. I had to admit that I was finding all the walking a tiny bit tedious. I began to question my motives. Was I just continuing out of stubbornness?

I wild camped on the springy twiggy heather on Pinhaw hill top. The countryside is very much managed moorland. I had walked through a couple of small villages and passed farms. It didn't feel very off grid and I was mindful that I might be stumbled upon, possibly by a dog walker, a farmer or a gamekeeper. Maybe it was just paranoia on my part, but it felt a long way from the Highlands on the Cape Wrath Trail.

Sunrise at May's.

Tent frost print.

Amongst the heather on Pinhaw hill top.

DAY 5

Pinhaw hill top to Water Houses
Weather: Sunny but chilly
17.5 miles
1600ft ascent

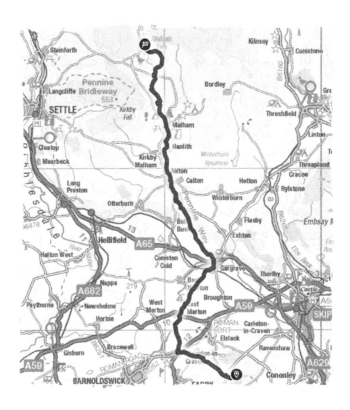

Another frosty morning and my stove spluttered and died just as the water for my morning tea and Readybrek had boiled. "Oh well," I thought, "it could have been worse; the gas could have given out before breakfast." The Way took me on through the villages of Thornton-in-Craven and East Marston. Both were quaint enough, but they boasted of no facilities for a weary wayfarer. If you are a lost goat, though, there is a goat sanctuary in Thornton-in-Craven, and if you are a bridge enthusiast, East Marston has a fine example of a double-arched bridge. I briefly walked alongside the Leeds to Liverpool canal and exchanged greetings with the friendly barge dwellers. I imagined we viewed each other as equally foreign entities.

The terrain I ambled through was all sheep-filled fields. It was spring after all and wee woolly critters were in abundance. Crossing a footbridge I saw a lamb in the stream below. Suspended, perfectly frozen mid gambol except for its lifeless eyes inches below the water, it was like some macabre Damien Hurst springtime art installation reflecting on the precipitous fragility of life. It left me feeling melancholic and in a sombre reflective mood for some time. It struck me that whilst spring in the countryside is full of life, there is also a great deal of death. And unlike in my usual human existence, death is not airbrushed out of everyday life.

In the metropolis that is Gargrave I restocked at the Co-op. The first Co-op on the route and (in hindsight) it turned out to be the best Co-op of the trip, with plentiful hot pasties. I was already tuning in to my body's preferred walking fare. Cheddar, peanuts and chocolate – readily available, dense, high-calorific foods that can happily last a few days in a backpack. I took advantage of a handily placed bench just outside the Co-op to eat lunch, pack supplies and discard as much surplus packaging as possible.

I phoned a nearby campsite hoping to get more gas. After a brief conversation the person on the phone shouted to their colleague: "It's one of those Pennine Wayers on the phone. Have we got any camping gas?" Alas, the answer that came back was a resounding no. Apparently they had had a run on gas canisters the previous weekend and as yet they had not had a chance to restock.

Between Gargrave and Airton I got a bit lost. One sheep-filled field looks much like another and once again waymarkers were sparse. It took a bit of ad libbing, crossing random fields and climbing walls and gates before I was back on track.

I passed some excellent wild camp spots next to the River Aire which, at that point, is more of a stream than a river. It was too early to stop so I continued north to Malham. Malham was a hive of activity and teeming with tourists. I made a swift exit and weaved my way up the majestic Malham Cove. There were plenty of climbers scaling its heights and as I watched, one fell off. I held my breath, but the tense instant lasted a fraction of a second as a rope took the tension of the falling climber. With his fall arrested, the climber scampered back up like Spider-Man. Even from a distance the climber's body language implied that he was frustrated more than scared by the fall. He must have had total faith in his safety rope. I'm not so sure that I would have been happy trusting my life to a single security line.

Malham Cove marks the beginning of wilder countryside. Farmland is replaced by natural fells. The scenery and views improve with each mile. I never get tired of the beautiful crazy geology of limestone pavement.

The Way took me around Malham Tarn, which was festooned with signs forbidding camping. A shame, I thought, as it was an ideal location and my legs were getting tired. I settled for filling up with water from the tarn. A little further north, at Water Houses, I stumbled upon a lovely spot to camp.

I was not far from a couple of houses, but up on a knoll I was hidden from the scant civilisation. I made camp on my tussocky perch and enjoyed a quiet evening.

The mighty Malham Cove.

Crazy limestone pavement above Malham Cove.

Perfect pitch at Water Houses.

DAY 6

Water Houses to Dodd Fell
Weather: Mostly sunny but chilly
18 miles
3200ft ascent

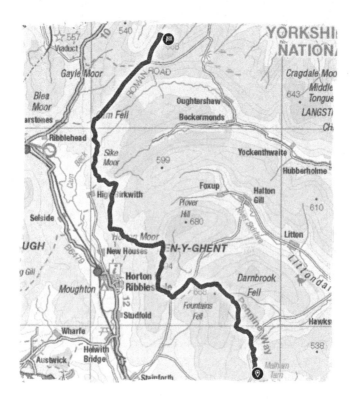

I upgraded my strategy from stuffing the gas canister down my sleeping bag to stuffing it up my down jacket. My additional body heat enabled me to coax a little more gas from the canister. Enough for a warming morning cuppa.

It was quite a long, beautiful early morning walk up to Fountains Fell. On the summit, which I find is more of a plateau, there were ominous signs warning that you should stay on the footpath or risk falling to your doom down open mine shafts. I investigated various holes but was unable to locate impenetrable doom in any of them. The views across to the Yorkshire Three Peaks were, however, uplifting.

Down dale then up Pen-y-ghent. I enjoyed the steep exhilarating ascent and paused for an olive ciabatta and houmous lunch on the summit. I then went down again into Ribble Dale. I avoided the loop south to Horton-in-Ribblesdale and took the Yorkshire Three Peaks path, which conveniently connects back with the Pennine Way a little further north. The diversion to Horton seemed pointless, as the village had nothing to offer the well-stocked wild camping wayfarer. Perhaps in non-Covid times I would have been drawn by the lure of a pub, a proper campsite and a hot shower. But alas such luxuries were out of bounds. I made do with stopping fleetingly to brew up beside a picturesque stream near Old Ing, where the water is swallowed by a dramatic dark hole.

Passing an impressive deep and narrow gorge at Ling Gill, I was duly informed by a notice board that it was a rare example of sub-alpine ash woodland of which there are only a handful left in Europe. There's a bridge just above the narrow ravine with an inscription stating it was repaired in 1765. I wondered how solid the repair work was as I gingerly crossed. It took the weight of me and my pack without grumbling. Not bad for a 256-year-old repair work.

That just left me with the inextricably slow climb along a forestry track up Dodd Fell. Fortunately it was not that steep as it was the third hill of the day, but it did continue for several hours. Once again, light winds allowed high camping and I cut off the Pennine Way in search of the top of the hill. Finding the terrain somewhat uneven and covered in clumps of grass I pragmatically sorted out a level spot just off the trig point. The 360° panoramic views were striking and I was treated to a sublime sunset.

It was another crisp night and I noticed my Platypus water bladder icing up. I put it in a dry bag and stuffed it down my sleeping bag. I woke in the early hours with an ominous sloshing in my bed. The water bladder had defrosted and leaked but fortunately the dry bag had saved me from a wet and cold disaster. It had contained the water and prevented me and my bed from getting drenched.

Hello Pen-y-ghent!

Ling Gill tea stop spot.

Sunset from the top of Dodd Fell.

DAY 7

Dodd Fell to Swaledale
Weather: Cold start then sunny
16.5 miles
2550ft ascent

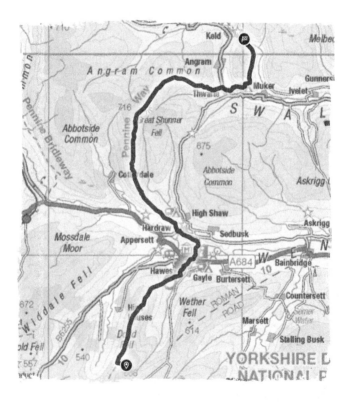

It was another frosty morning up on Dodd Fell and possibly my coldest yet at -5°C. I was relieved to encourage the final bit of gas out of the canister for a morning Readybrek and hot chocolate. Between almost boiling water for my drink and porridge I had to warm the canister next to my skin to encourage the isobutane/propane to change from liquid back to its functional gaseous state – a bracing experience, but worth it in return for a hot breakfast. It was a beautiful, clear, blue sky day and bristlingly cold with it. I continued my regime of scraping ice off the tent before packing it away, and then I threw in a few star jumps for good measure to maintain warmth between bouts of frosty scraping.

I enjoyed a gentle two-hour amble down to Hawes. My peace and reverie were rudely shattered by a couple of pairs of fast jet fly boys playing aerial tag in the valley below ridge height.

In Hawes I first headed to the post office, which I found tucked away down an alley. Hawes post office is also the tourist office, library and community centre. Fortunately, my resupply parcel had arrived so I was restocked with Readybrek and, more importantly, gas. I made good use of a sunny bench just outside to do a stock take and pack my new acquisitions. I then tracked down the butcher's for a sandwich, sausage roll and pasty, plus some orange juice for a hit of Vitamin C. I snaffled it all on the sunny, quiet bench outside the post office. Next stop was the Spar for bread, houmous, Cheddar, peanuts, chocolate and wine. Again I made use of the bench outside the post office to pack supplies. Noting that sadly my water bladder was now defunct and not salvageable,

I kept the single-use drinks bottles to use as a makeshift stand-in. Restocked, packed and prepped for at least two days, I departed and strolled north to Hardraw.

Half a mile before the village that is mainly known for its waterfall, which I considered was probably more of a water trickle as it had been so dry, I stepped through a gate into the next field of many on the route. I was confronted by a nervous, but no doubt proud, new mum who had just given birth. A lamb lay in a gooey heap and mum was busy licking mucus membrane gunk from her offspring. I'm not sure who was more surprised. I spoke in what I hoped were soothing congratulatory tones and softly went on my way.

Surveying the map I decided that water sources would be scarce up on Great Shunner Fell, so I retrieved a litre of fresh spring water from a stream on my way out of Hardraw. Recalling the dead lamb in the stream from two days ago, I was mindful to filter the water. I resisted the draw of the waterfall/dribble and started up the steady rise of the next hill at hand. The additional water made my already weighty resupplied pack even heavier. The walk up Great Shunner Fell was a two-hour slog. The sun was shining and the temperature was maybe just nudging double figures. The gentle breeze and altitude made it feel more like mid-single figures. Despite the coolness I had stripped away and stowed my outer layers.

I'm not sure why, considering the drudgery of that climb, but it was somewhere along that ascent that I changed my mind about journaling this walk. I had initially decided not to. It had felt a bit normal, repeating how I had felt on previous walks. So far, walking the Pennine Way, I hadn't really found my mojo. But plodding up Great

Shunner Fell I remembered why I do these things. I forgot about logistics and daily mileage. Mentally, after six days, I found my stride. A kind of inner peace tuning into the metronome of life.

Atop the fell I absorbed the all-round views of the Yorkshire Dales. The landscape was visceral and devoid of civilisation. I celebrated the summit with two cups of tea. This refreshed me and lightened my load. I lingered for an hour with the hill to myself, slurping down the tea and drinking in the views. Checking in with my body, I found that my legs, knees and feet all felt good. I floated as much as walked down the other side of the fell towards Thwaite. Even where parts of the path were tricky going, with loose tennis ball size irregular stones underfoot, I picked my way through with relative ease.

As already mentioned, the Pennine Way is economically signposted. Maybe the National Trails authority had run out of money? Maybe they thought it was such an established route that it didn't need marking? Maybe locals had used the finger posts as firewood? Maybe souvenir hunting wayfarers had taken them as trophies? To say that Pennine Way signs were sparse would be generous. In parts I began to think that finding a steaming pile of rocking horse poop would be more likely. Or maybe a real live rainbow unicorn? In hindsight I think the National Trails authority felt that navigating the Pennine Way has to be earned, and if you cannot read a map you are not welcome.

After taking a couple of false exits out of Thwaite I was briefly back on track. Heading up the fells round to Keld, ten minutes later I came to a gate with a hand-painted sign on it. It read, "Hello :-) Sorry, but this is not the Pennine Way :-(." I appreciated the sad face emoji and took solace in the fact that I wasn't the first wayfarer to have made this navigational error; hence the need for the sign.

After a bit of backtracking I was back on the route, rounding the hills into the stunning Swaledale valley. It was sublimely picturesque and atmospheric, like the land that time forgot. Shunner Fell was OK, but I was surprised it was named "Great" Shunner Fell. If the locals were so impressed by their surrounding landscape, I'm disappointed they didn't name Swaledale as the "Most Awesome Swaledale".

I wild camped in a ravine next to the River Swale, a mile or so from Keld and a short walk from Kisdon Force waterfall. I spotted a brood of ducklings faithfully following their mum through the eddies and currents of the river like little feathery pingpong balls bobbing up and down. There was one straggler taking detours and missing the best lines through the water course. I decide that his name was probably the duck equivalent of Nigel.

Proud mum and her new arrival.

The Most Awesome Swaledale.

DAY 8

Swaledale to Blackton Reservoir
Weather: Cold start then sunny
15 miles
1700ft ascent

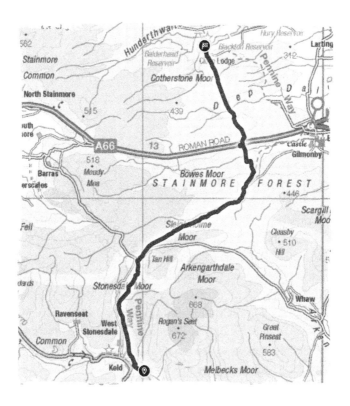

I packed up and enjoyed a lovely sunny morning stroll along the River Swale past Kisdon Force and Catrake Force waterfalls. Then I headed up across Stonedale Moor to the Tan Hill Inn. My morning walking was my favourite time of the day. The world felt fresh, and due to the early hour I had it to myself.

I arrived at the Tan Hill Inn, the UK's highest pub at 1,732ft above sea level, at 10.30am. I had to admit that its position didn't feel particularly lofty and I put that down to the fact that I'd been travelling over a few hills recently. Other hills did feel reasonably high with corresponding resplendent views, whereas the views around the inn were of rolling moorland. Although it didn't occur to me at the time, the inn also marked the halfway point of my Pennine Way route. My morning arrival was unfortunately an hour and a half before the kitchen opened. On expressing my dismay at the lack of food opportunities, the helpful bar staff called the kitchen, who accommodatingly knocked me up a bacon butty.

As I was sitting in the sunshine waiting for my second breakfast to arrive, I went to plug my phone into the solar panel. Disaster! I discovered that my charger cable was missing! I emptied and searched my pack but found nothing. I realised that I must have left the charger cable back where I'd camped. I remembered carefully coiling it up and placing it on my map case just before I struck camp that morning. Once packed up I must have picked up my map case letting the cable fall to the ground unnoticed. My phone had perhaps two or three days' charge left in it if I used it carefully, but I was still at least a week off finishing the walk. How could I communicate with my family?

How could I plan my extraction? How could I check the weather? How could I check my navigation? What about checking the news and listening to music? In that moment I realised just how useful and comforting my phone was to me. I entertained the idea of the four-hour round trip walk to return to my camp spot. As I paid my bill I explained my dilemma and asked the staff at the inn if anyone had a spare USB C cable I could have. I felt it was a long shot, but minutes later I was presented with a cable and they refused to take payment for it. I put £10 in the Mountain Rescue collection box and thanked my guardian angel.

Ironically, on walking the Pennine Way so far, I had come across a number of accidentally discarded items, ranging from hats and gloves to a fleece I had passed that very morning, and even a pair of boxer shorts a few days earlier. They had probably fallen unknowingly from a pack. I had wondered how sad their owners would have been upon discovering the loss of their possessions. Now I knew first hand and it took me a moment to gather my wits. Over the last few minutes I had experienced a whole gamut of emotions. Starting with anger at my stupidity then moving swiftly on to loss, regret, annoyance, fear and acceptance. Having acquired a new cable, my feelings switched to joy, gratitude and thankfulness. I must have looked flustered and in need of all the help I could get, as another of the staff at the Tan Hill Inn came and gave me a complimentary energy bar before I left. They wished me good luck. I reckoned I'd be needing it.

The next stretch of the Way was towards the busy A66. I could see and hear the road in the distance. The way was very soggy underfoot and that was after the long spell of dry weather. I was pretty sure it wouldn't have been much fun crossing Sleightholme Moor during more typical wet weather. I suspect that moor would be high on the list destined for the stone flagging treatment that many parts of the Pennine Way had succumbed to. Paradoxically, whilst I didn't enjoy having wet feet, squelching with each footstep, I felt it would be a shame to tame all the boggy sections of the Way.

I arrived on the other side of the moor at God's Bridge. I had seen it marked on the map and had been wondering what to expect. The bridge was something of an anticlimax given its celestial name but it made a good place to stop for lunch. I contemplated the bridge whilst snaffling cheese and bread. On closer inspection of the bridge it appeared to be a natural structure with the softer rock below maybe having been eroded away by the water flow over millennia. A natural fluke of geology. Perhaps that was why the bridge acquired its name?

I made use of the underwhelming but safe underpass to traverse the slightly scary A66 with all its frenetic traffic. I pondered for a moment where everyone was going and what was the rush? The Way continued north over the Great Allotment. I noted that there were no brassicas to be found. In fact I struggled to find a path or anything much beyond grass tussocks and spongy wet moss for several hours. Having lost the path for the umpteenth time I decided it was easier just to walk on a compass bearing until I got to the other side. Navigationally my plan was sound but it involved an hour of me schlepping across soggy balls of marsh grass on challenging moor. Not the most fun terrain.

Eventually I made it to a tarmac track and Clove Lodge, which was definitely on the Pennine Way according to the map. But which gate to exit? I find my navigation is weakest passing through farmyards and villages when I'm presented with an array of options. With no signs or clues available to give me a hint of the correct exit, once again I was struggling to believe I was walking the UK's first and most well-known national trail. I chose gate number two which took me generally the right way. After zigzagging a couple of fields, I stumbled upon a finger post, which assured me that I wasn't totally lost.

I had planned to walk further, but there was a perfect camp spot next to a babbling brook that flowed into Blackton Reservoir. After all the tussock hopping, my feet were grumbling, so at just after 5pm I pitched my tent. I scoffed a hearty chorizo and couscous dinner washed down with a fine Merlot, while soaking up a perfect, gentle, sunny spring evening.

On passing the Tan Hill Inn, in my fluster over the lost cable, I had barely registered that it represented the halfway mark of this walk. That evening I did notice that the number of map tiles I had were beyond the halfway mark and were now diminishing. It had taken me seven days to mentally find my stride. To my surprise my body had coped physically very well from the outset. And now it felt like I was within grasp of achieving what I had set out to do – almost finished, almost done, just as I was getting warmed up!

Neat drystone walling.

Blackton Reservoir camp.

DAY 9

Blackton Reservoir to High Cup Nick
Weather: Cold start then sunny
23.5 miles
2550ft ascent

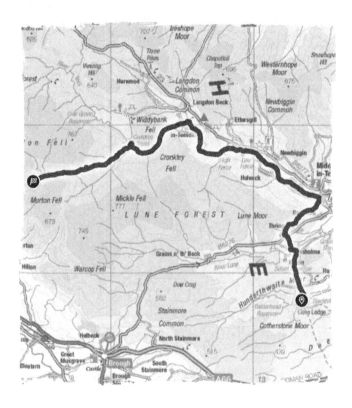

Another peaceful night's sleep, yawn. My left foot was sore from yesterday afternoon's tussock hopping and general soggy bog sliding exertions. On inspection I couldn't see anything obviously wrong with my heel, as the skin there was dry and thick. I thought perhaps there was a crack in the skin so I applied an Asda imitation Compeed plaster. I was on my way by 7.30am, hoping to make good time and conscious of my short previous day. But I delayed departure until I had applied my new routine of thoroughly checking that I had left nothing behind, especially any rogue cables.

I continued to be lucky with the stunning weather. Light wind, sunshine and refreshingly cool. I soon passed another couple of reservoirs which I'd been unsure about continuing on to the previous day as I wasn't sure about their wild camping viability. It was part of the reason I had stopped a little early, along with the sore foot. These reservoirs were much more public with a car park and a toilet. There were at least a dozen fishermen there at 8.30am. I had often found in my experience of wild camping on long distance walks that the best camping spot is generally the one I had just passed or the one I didn't quite get to. On this occasion I decided that camping there would have been doable but the spot was nowhere near as nice as where I had actually decided to stay the night.

I meandered through a couple of farmyards and over the tops across Lune Moor. The signposting was again a tad vague. I was helped back on track by a friendly gamekeeper, who also gave me fresh water from an outside tap on his house. This made for a refreshing change from my more usual practice of filtering river water. I stopped on Crossthwaite Common to brew up and finish off my bread and cheese before I made a resupply stop at the upcoming town, Middleton-in-Teesdale.

Middleton-in-Teesdale is a reasonably sized town and offered a variety of eating options including cafes, restaurants, pizza, and fish and chips. Once again, my time of arrival was poor. At mid-morning all the copious eatery options were closed. I made do with the Co-op and bought a meal deal sandwich/snack/drink plus my usual supplies of bread, milk, houmous, peanuts, chocolate and wine. Making use of an ideally located bench in town, I decanted the wine into my lightweight plastic bottles and discarded the glass bottle and as much of the food packaging as possible. Not wanting to linger in the town, I headed on with my now well-burdened pack in search of a peaceful picnic spot for lunch. The Way meandered along the banks of the mostly level and scenic River Tees. I found a bucolic corner, where I soaked my feet in the river and ate my lunch.

On a walk like this I tend to lose track of time and days passing, but it slowly dawned on me that it was a Saturday. The weekend fine weather meant the place was crawling with grockles. "How dare other people clutter up my scenery," I harrumphed as I passed Low Force and High Force waterfalls. The heel of my left foot also continued to complain but not about the tourists. I put my physical discomfort down to the inferior Asda plaster that I had used. The pain didn't help my mood. Mid-afternoon, just beyond Cronkley, which sounded like a fine adjective for my current disposition, I stopped for another brew by the River Tees. Inspecting my foot I discovered two things.

70

First was that the problem wasn't a cracked heel but definitely a blister, which was now quite well developed. The second was that I had managed to put the Asda fake Compeed plaster next to the blister and not over it, which explained the increasing pain. I deployed an original Compeed plaster in the correct location. Instant relief.

Looking at the map I realised I was getting within spitting distance of High Cup Nick. I had read that it was arguably the most jaw-dropping part of the Pennine Way, and it was part of the UK that I hadn't already experienced. It would make for a long day, but I reckoned it would be worth the effort to see it at sunset and sunrise. And it would be an amazing place to camp. I put my socks and boots back on and ploughed on, my foot much happier for the Compeed.

Again I took the wrong route somewhere and walked the wrong way, but this time I bumped into a heard of friendly Highland cows before I realised my navigational error. "Not all wrong turns are bad wrong turns," I thought before correcting my direction.

The countryside was becoming wilder and the number of people I passed diminished sharply. I did come across a couple of bird watchers, each furtively clutching a pair of binoculars. I enquired as to whether they knew the name of an orange-beaked black and white bird that had caught my attention and I had seen quite a few of. I was sure it wasn't a lapwing, as that was one of a few birds I did know. It was, however, quite distinctive and I described it as a slimmer version of a penguin that could fly. I don't think the penguin reference was constructive, but helpfully the bird in question appeared nearby. I pointed it out, "That one over there," I declared. Apparently it was an oyster catcher. I wasn't sure if the twitchers were making fun of me as I felt we were a long way from any oysters. Since returning home and googling "oyster catcher" I now know it was indeed an oyster catcher. And I stand by my flying penguin reference. Look it up yourself if you don't believe me.

Following Maize Brook around to Cauldron Snout the terrain underfoot was rocky and torturous. By contrast my surroundings were glorious. Something West Highland-esque about it. Visceral, wild and stunning. I loved it. I had plugged myself into my dance tunes playlist to help me maintain a good pace and as I rounded a bend in the river I was met by the full force of Cauldron Snout – a thunderous cascade just below the dam of Cow Green Reservoir. Coldplay's "Every teardrop is a waterfall" was playing at that moment, exactly at the part of the song where Chris Martin sings, "It's a waterfall! Ahhh..." over and over. "It certainly is," I thought to myself.

Above Cauldron Snout I bumped into a chap who was carrying a fluffy toy dog in an outside pocket of his backpack, which I commented on. We got chatting and introduced ourselves. His name was Rob and the fluffy toy dog was in memory of a friend who had died recently. Rob was local to these parts and was planning on walking the Pennine Way in a couple of months. He was a bit concerned about wild camping and I was able to reassure him that it wouldn't present a major problem. In turn he assured me that High Cup Nick was under two hours away and that I should comfortably make it before sunset. We wished each other well and parted our ways.

Spurred on by more dance tunes, I floated across the

fells. The miles fell away beneath my boots. A couple of hours later I arrived at High Cup Nick. I can confirm that it is truly spectacular. I raised my arms in the air, gave a whoop of joy and did a dad dance jig celebrating my arrival at this breathtaking awe-inspiring natural venue. I had been vaguely concerned that it wouldn't live up to its hype but it did not disappoint. The size and symmetry of the place is spectacular. And, even better, I had arrived before sunset. Probably quite fortunately considering my dancing skills, I had the place to myself. I had thought that, as it was a Saturday and with the weather so accommodating, it might be teeming with other folk up there enjoying the views.

As I swung my backpack down, my elation was abruptly cut short when my pack yanked my earphones wires. The wires were severed. I now unintentionally had wireless earbuds. The music stopped. "Oops," I thought, "Should have unplugged them." Still, the epicness of my surroundings didn't allow me to berate myself too much or for my mood to be dimmed.

I pitched my tent a few feet from the edge of the precipitous drop into the valley. This was one of my most dramatic camps ever. I sipped red wine and cooked up pancetta, which I had in a wrap with houmous. I absorbed the atmosphere. There was even some phone reception, so I was able to message family and friends. Lovely wine. Lovely sunset. Feet throbbing. Maybe it was time to deploy the ibuprofen?

Soaking my feet in the River Tees.

How now brown cow?

Above Cauldron Snout.

Weary feet above High Cup Nick.

High Cup Nick camp.

DAY 10

High Cup Nick to River South Tyne near Garrigill
Weather: Grey and overcast
20 miles
2700ft ascent

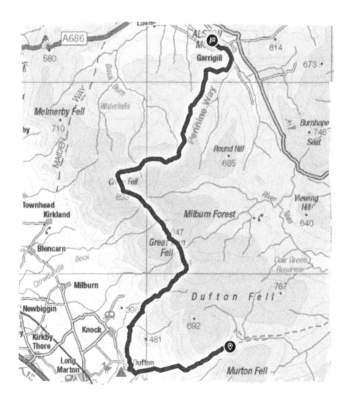

Yet another peaceful night's sleep, yawn, up on High Cup Nick with no wind. How lucky could I get? And the first morning that I didn't need to scrape ice off the tent. The cracked heel was clearly a blister, so I operated on it. Piercing the blister with a scalpel blade, I drained it of fluid and then applied a new Compeed plaster. It felt much less painful. I packed up and moseyed down to Dufton, passing four friendly magnificent wild ponies.

Down on the plains, Dufton turned out to be a small village with very little to it. Allegedly there was a hostel, campsite, pub and shop in normal times. Perhaps the place is more happening when it's not 9am on a Sunday morning? Especially not during a pandemic? When I passed through, there were mainly lovely country houses with Range Rovers and Porsches parked on their driveways. To me, Dufton seemed quite a detour for very little benefit. I was soon striding through farmland and on my way back up onto the fells.

I stopped around 10am for a second breakfast – more houmous and bread – and I indulged in my first ibuprofen of the walk. My throbbing feet and stinging blister settled down to a subdued background hum of annoyance. I continued up to the NATS (National Air Traffic Services) golf ball radar on Great Dun Fell. Considering that I had seen this landmark from afar, it felt disappointingly small and unimpressive up close. Just beyond there I spotted a stoat. Or was it a weasel? Not sure which, but I know my dad would tell me, "Weasels are weasily recognisable and stoats are stoatally different..." boom, boom... On Little Dun Fell, at 1pm, I stopped for tea, taking advantage of a handily placed horseshoe-shaped summit shelter to hide from the wind.

The all-round views were of the fells but their grandeur was subdued and the colours washed out due to an overcast hazy sky. Onwards to Cross Fell, apparently the highest point of the Pennine Way. Cross Fell has such a large, flat summit that it obscures the surrounding scenery, but it does boast a magnificent cairn with north/south/east/west sheltered seating areas. Having just stopped and brewed up on the hillock before, there was no reason to dawdle, so I continued with little ceremony, down and round past Greg's Hut, a Mountain Bothies Association bothy. I have been very grateful of a well-placed bothy in my past meanderings, but this time round the fair weather and the early time of day meant I did not need its services. I peaked inside to find it empty, save for a table, a few chairs and a string of Tibetan prayer flags.

The remainder of the afternoon was spent traipsing along a dull gravel track that snaked down to Garrigill. I was buoyed on by the possibility of a Sunday roast at a pub in the village. Alas, on arrival, the only pub in Garrigill was closed and looked like it had been for some time. Through dusty windows I could make out chairs stacked upside down upon tables. I exited the village along the River South Tyne and within a mile I found a lovely spot to camp nestled on the banks of the river.

I tried to plan the last four days of the walk plus my extraction. I still had a significant number of miles to cover. A few days ago my wife had asked me if I was enjoying the walk and, being honest with myself, there and then, I wasn't so sure. I enjoyed the wild camping and some of the wilder countryside, but much of the walking had been plain boring. My feet now hurt, I was in need of a shower, and my clothes needed a wash. I was pushing merino wool's anti-bacterial properties to the limit. My socks were beginning to whiff. It would have been great to get a pub meal, but in Covid times such opportunities were limited.

On the plus side it was noticeably warmer. And in times when I was struggling mentally, it was important for me to value any and all plus points of my current situation. It was yet another beautiful evening. I took a deep breath, soaked up the babbling river, the ambience and the sunset. "Really?" I thought to myself, "Except for having my family with me to share the moment with, I don't think I could ask for more."

Morning on High Cup Nick.

Friendly wild pony.

Camping next to the River South Tyne.

DAY 11

River South Tyne near Garrigill to Hadrian's Wall
Weather: Dry and partly cloudy
22 miles
1570ft ascent

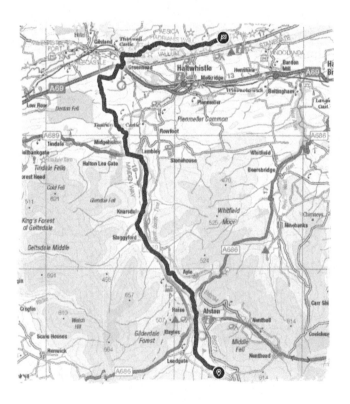

Yet another (yawn, double yawn) peaceful night by the river, and it was warm. There was no scraping ice off the tent today. There was also no sign of any dog walkers, despite my close proximity to population, but perhaps my early rising routine trumped even the most diligent of hound owners. I was awake at 4am, which hadn't been uncommon on this walk but it still surprised me. I was generally asleep not long after 9pm most nights, but I had hoped that with all the exercise I was doing my body would want more than seven hours' sleep. Still, the upside was witnessing the day slowly come to life and the first few hours' walking were some of my favourite of the day.

Looking at my schedule I reckoned I was on course to get to the end of my walk along the Pennine Way, Kirk Yetholm, a day earlier than planned. My family hadn't been able to find any reasonably priced accommodation options near Kirk Yetholm and Scotland was still officially closed, so the need for me to extract myself was looking increasingly likely. From what I had read, getting from Kirk Yetholm back home by public transport was not a swift or easy feat. I really didn't relish the idea of spending over six hours on buses and trains. A strange thought occurred to me, "What about walking home?" I felt it was an odd idea on several levels. Firstly, until very recently, I had been feeling ambivalent about my whole Pennine Way experience. Secondly, walking 250 miles is quite a long way, but to walk 500 miles is just insane. Then there was the high possibility that my wife and my children wouldn't be very happy with me being away for at least another week if not two. Apart from that, could my body, knees and feet endure the continued abuse?

My spirits soared as I walked along the River South Tyne in the morning light through rolling fields full of ewes and their abundant bouncy lambs. The day was still with not a breath of wind. Above and around were a crystal clear pale blue sky. The burbling river at my side, baa-ing sheep, bird song and the odd woodpecker were my soundtrack. I paused for a moment and took advantage of a thoughtfully placed bench in the middle of a field. Soaking up the views and absorbing a little serenity, I felt that anything was possible.

I arrived in Alston an hour before the post office opened. This was where I was due to pick up my second supply parcel so I had some time to kill. I regretted breaking my earbuds, as I had many days, if not weeks, of walking ahead of me, so I was delighted to find earbuds for sale in the Spar. Result! I had music again!

I also bought a family pack of ham from the Spar for my second breakfast. I was a little disappointed that there was no hot food to be had, but what could I expect at 9am on a Monday morning. I called my wife and mentioned my new slightly crazy idea of walking home. Her instant response was laughter. Quite a lot of laughter, bordering on hysterical. Once her mirth had subsided, I explained my logic. I reasoned that any fool could walk the Pennine Way but it would take a special kind of fool to walk it there and back. She did agree with that. Especially the "fool" bit. She conceded that if that was what I wanted to do, then now was as good an opportunity as ever. I left it that she would talk to the girls and see how we all felt about it in a day or so.

I supplemented my resupply provisions with minimal additional rations from the Spar as I reckoned I would make it to Bellingham, the next town on the route, by late afternoon the following day. Studying my map I decided that the Pennine Way did a fair amount of unnecessary wiggling and decided to walk on the slightly more direct River Tyne Trail. This followed an old railway line that ran along the river and rejoined the Way at Slaggyford five miles away. The day was turning out to be warm, so I stripped off and plugged myself into a playlist, walking through picturesque, but rurally manicured, scenery.

My little solar panel continued to work brilliantly, keeping my phone fully charged. Usefully, the Pennine Way does run south to north, so most of the time the sun was on my back and the solar panel clipped onto my backpack. Without the solar panel I wouldn't have been able to make as much use of my phone to message, listen to music, take pictures and check navigation. Listening to music meant that potentially dull hours of walking slipped by painlessly – so much so that I sailed through Slaggyford and had walked another five miles before I realised I should have been back on the Pennine Way.

My newly purchased earbuds stopped working on the west side at Lambley viaduct. I cursed their inferior build quality, but in hindsight this was probably a good thing; otherwise I might have kept walking on that trail till its end. I took the cessation of music in my left ear as a signal to stop for a break. I also took the combination of the sunshine and my location on the banks of the River South Tyne as a sign that perhaps I should wash myself and my clothes. Besides, if I was going to walk home again, I couldn't go over three weeks without washing. Even for my dubious hygiene standards, that was getting ridiculous.

The water was bracing. Actually, it was glacial. But after splashing my face, head and neck I was able to submerge myself without going into cold shock. Nevertheless my wash was brisk. Once dried and dressed I returned to the river and did a rudimentary wash of my socks, boxer shorts and base layer. I then had a late lunch lazing in the sunshine and restoring my core body temperature.

I rejoined the Pennine Way with my washing tied to the outside of my pack drying in the sun. This included my only pair of boxer shorts so at that point I was "going commando". I hoped I wouldn't experience excessive chafing. Any thought of bodily discomfort was soon erased as I was confronted with a field of a dozen or so heavy set stocky cows all loitering on the path. I wondered if the Pennine Way was punishing me for my infidelity with The South Tyne Trail. I also wondered if the cows were bulls, but then noticed another cow alone in the next field with a ring through its nose. I deduced that the cows in my immediate way were lady cows but they were still nonetheless rather large lady cows and that made me nervous. It's a fact that cows are the most dangerous animal in the UK. The Health and Safety Executive note that cows are responsible for an average of four to five deaths a year. Lone walkers tend to be the victims. As I approached the cattle they did move but were a tad skittish for comfort given their tonne bulk. Once beyond my nemeses I relaxed a little, crossing low level marshland which would usually have been very wet. Again I was grateful for the spell of dry weather that saved me from the worst of the Pennine Way boggy obstacles.

A little further on I came to Greenriggs, a farm that

looked like it had seen better days. The Way passed through the front yard, home to a shabby caravan, a fire pit and a pile of empty Stella cans. There was a hand-painted sign offering refreshments and I wondered what might be on offer. Rounding the house to the back I came across a bald potbellied man in his fifties sporting a discoloured white skin-tight vest. He was hand carving a crooked medieval looking five-foot-long axe handle. The axe head itself was rusty, double sided and about the size of a large shoe box. Next to him was an enormous pile of empty Stella cans that could have easily hidden your average family hatchback.

It was quite a tableau and reminiscent of a hillbilly scene from a Northumberland version of Deliverance. As he noticed me, he stopped his whittling, straightened up and reached for a can of Stella, from which he took a long gulp. His teeth were stained yellow and his eyes focused somewhere above and beyond my left shoulder. I wondered whether after murdering me he would eat my liver and make my skin into a pair of chaps? We exchanged greetings and he asked if I would like any refreshments, offering me the choice of Stella, Irn-Bru or Red Bull. I declined. Alas, he was all out of orange juice. We got talking, and despite outward appearances he was an affable fellow. He introduced himself as Rastaman Ralph and explained he'd moved to the house a couple of years earlier in complete ignorance of the Pennine Way that ran through his yard. It was only when walkers kept passing by and told him about the national trail that he realised his property was on the oldest long distance walking route in the UK. He kept himself busy looking after a small menagerie of animals. He offered me a free place to camp for the night, but as it was only 4pm I said it was too early. I bid him farewell and continued on my way, with my liver and skin intact.

Observing that the Way doglegged around the perimeter of a large scrub field, I decided to take the direct line diagonally across it, only to find myself ankle deep in bog. I backtracked and scolded myself for my foolishness. Somewhere traversing that field the right earbud stopped working. My meagre source of music had given up altogether. So much for the Spar headphones.

Approaching Hadrian's Wall, walking across Haltwhistle golf course, a greenskeeper came trundling towards me on a John Deere mower. I thought I was going to be told off for trespassing and preempted hostilities with a hearty hello before enquiring if I was on the right path. Apparently, I was not on the right path, but the man was very friendly and happily explained where I should be. He even offered me refreshments at the clubhouse despite my washing still fluttering on my backpack. I thanked him and declined, as I wanted to make a little further progress along Hadrian's Wall to find a camp spot.

I passed a row of houses before cutting up towards Thirlwall Castle. Anticipating that Tipalt Burn might be dryish and probably less than savoury as a source of water, I approached a bloke who was minding his own business pottering in his garden and asked if I could possibly have some water. He barely batted an eyelid as I handed him my random assortment of bottles to fill up. Prepped and prepared for the evening ahead, I started to follow the wall. I have visited Hadrian's Wall before, but as a passing day tripper. This time I was looking forward to properly absorbing the atmosphere and camping on the demarcation line where the Romans had decided to make a firm stand against the Picts. I had barely walked a mile before I passed a couple of young lads hauling very large backpacks including a bulky pop-up tent swinging off one of their packs. I asked if they'd passed any potential camp spots and they said that the terrain was wilder a mile or two further on. They were walking the Hadrian's Wall Path. They had been on the go for a few days and clearly suffering from their fair complexion combined with walking east to west. They had endured an unseasonal amount of sun. Both were severely sunburnt on their left side. I suggested they walk the route back again to even up the exposure, but they seemed to have had enough sun for the moment.

I walked further than I had wanted to before I found a spot where I felt I was sufficiently out of the way for a calm night. It was yet another stunning location. I felt privileged to camp on such a historic monument. I made myself as discrete as possible, not wanting to show any disrespect for the historical site. I found a tucked away corner to pitch up and enjoyed lardons with couscous. Just as I was dropping off I heard an odd bird cawing. Maybe it was the ghosts and night ghasts of histories past? It didn't stop me drifting off to sleep, with more miles having been trodden underfoot.

A white acorn marking the Pennine Way.

Hadrian's Wall.

DAY 12

Hadrian's Wall to Hazel Burn
Weather: Cold start then sunny
21 miles
2000ft ascent

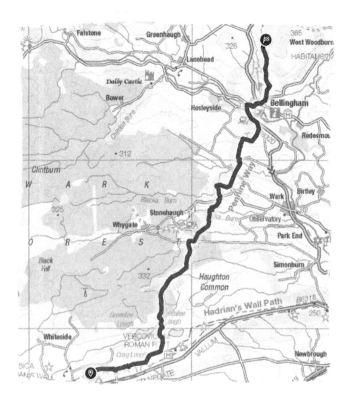

A peaceful night's sleep and I was not murdered by marauding Picts or ghostly centurions. I was on the road by 7.15am, conscious that I wanted to get to Bellingham in time to pick up my final resupply parcel from the post office, which shut at 5pm. It was a still, overcast morning. I was warmed by the many ups and downs as I continued to follow Hadrian's Wall. Much of the original wall has gone and been replaced by a rather unconvincing dry stone walling. I was doubtful of this as a defensive structure. However, there was one section where I was able to walk on top of the original wall, treading in the footsteps of the Romans just under 2000 years ago. I had the whole place to myself, only passing a couple of other walkers in three hours.

At Turret 37A I left the wall behind and resumed my northerly pilgrimage. Crossing moorland between Greenlee and Broomlee Loughs, I found a small gurgling stream, where I retrieved water and brewed up. Once rehydrated, I continued cautiously, re-routing round a cow and her calf a few fields on before I disappeared into dense commercial forest along cinder tracks. I fleetingly popped out of the woodland across Haughton Common before another spell of forestry schlepping.

Passing Horneystead Farm, which my pre-walk research informed me had snacks, I met Helen, the resident farmer. She welcomed me warmly. I discovered that she was a keen walker, having done the Pennine Way, Southern Upland Way and even the PCT. The PCT, or Pacific Crest Trail, is over two and a half thousand miles long stretching from Mexico to Canada along the west side of the USA. Helen showed me the walkers' "Pit Stop", a ramshackle outbuilding that offered snacks and cold drinks. The cold drinks were especially welcome on the warm afternoon. There was also what I had begun to recently dream about – a shower. I washed myself twice and thanked Helen for her hospitality before continuing on my way.

I arrived in Bellingham at just after 4pm, well before the post office was due to close and was reunited with my final supply parcel. I liberated two delicious pies (chicken curry and chicken and mushroom) and a sandwich from the local bakery, and purchased a bottle of Merlot from the Co-op. I took advantage of a village bench for my feast. I checked in with my family to see if I had the go ahead to walk home. They told me, with a hint of resignation, that if that's what I really want to do, then OK. I interpreted that as code for, "OK, but you're gonna pay later!"

I took stock and restocked accordingly. It was at least a day and a half to Kirk Yetholm and I was not sure if it had a shop. I calculated that it would be three to four days before I would be back in Bellingham. I bought more dry roasted peanuts, houmous, Cheddar, bread and chocolate. Fuelled on pies and wine I walked a good few more miles to find a sheltered camp spot at Hazel Burn.

On the way I passed a finger post signposting an "Alternative Pennine Way" and wondered if that was a version where someone else carried your bag, you got to stay in B&Bs and there is unlimited champagne on tap. Maybe next time, I promised myself.

Many ups and downs following Hadrian's Wall.

That tree from Robin Hood: Prince of Thieves.

Alternative Pennine Way anyone?

DAY 13

Hazel Burn to Windy Gyle
Weather: Overcast start, then sunny with a cooling breeze
26 miles
3000ft ascent

Awake again at 4.30am and again I wondered why I
didn't sleep longer after walking over 20 miles a day. It
was a cool, overcast morning as I crossed the heather-
covered rolling moors of Whitley Pike. At Padon Hill
the sun broke through the clouds making the morning
much warmer and the cooling easterly breeze became
quite welcome. Having had a long chat with my family the
previous day, my phone charge had dropped to 60%, the
lowest on the walk so far, but with the sun now bright and
squarely on my back the solar panel did its thing and my
phone was soon recharging swiftly.

After Brownrigg Head I was back into commercial
forest territory, as well as arboreal carnage where a section
had recently been harvested. Logging lorry tracks are
hard on the feet but swift to walk along. I dispatched
a map tile, covering six miles, in under two hours. My
quickest yet. From experience I knew it could take me
anything up to four hours to cross a map tile. The speed
I crossed a tile depended on two factors. The first is how
directly the route traverses the map. A route zigzagging
diagonally across the page is significantly less direct than
a route running straight north-south or east-west. The
second factor affecting speed is the terrain underfoot.
Bog hopping across sodden moors is much slower than
strolling across grassy meadows or plodding along forestry
cinder tracks, and scaling a steep rocky hillside also tends
to diminish my pace.

Crossing the River Rede I stopped at a thoughtfully
placed picnic table for a brew. A little further on I passed a
caravan and campsite with a sign offering camping and hot
showers for wayfarers for £10. I suspected the offer wasn't

currently valid. Covid restrictions only allowed caravans and camper vans to stay at campsites as they have their own showers and toilets. Besides, I had showered the day before and it was barely 1pm, so there was no time to stop.

Noting that water sources were likely to be scarce up on the Cheviots, I filled my collection of bottles from the river. The water looked a little brown and my Sawyer water filter was sluggish as it was in need of a clean. Arriving at Byrness, the last point of civilisation before Kirk Yetholm, I found it consisted of nothing more than a handful of houses and a church. Spotting a local person busy in their garden, I asked if perhaps I could have some water. She happily obliged, so I poured the river water I had collected onto a clump of daffodils before having them refilled with fresh tap water.

After a short steep climb I was soon up onto the tops where the sun was out in full force. Again, I was grateful for the cooling easterly breeze. The going was good due to the continued dry spell. The boggy bits were easily manageable and the ground springy. I barely needed the flagstones and boarded sections. There was a part of the path where the flagstones looked like the bog had swallowed them up and then spat them out. They were all higgledy piggledy. A nod to what conditions could be like. Yet again I counted my lucky stars for the unseasonably dry conditions.

The Way followed the perimeter of a military danger area and there were signs up warning me not to touch any military debris as it might explode and kill me. Clear and to the point. And duly noted. The Way passed a Roman Fort, marked on the map, which I thought would be an interesting place to stop for refreshments. Unfortunately, at least to my untrained eye, there wasn't much to see, just a series of lumps and ditches marking the place where the fort once stood. My hot chocolate was nonetheless very tasty. I was pleased that I had had the foresight to bring water with me, as the burns I found were slow flowing and close to stagnant.

At 2.30pm my feet were beginning to throb uncomfortably. Due to my stinginess I hadn't bought more ibuprofen in Bellingham, as all that was available was Nurofen and I balked at paying five times the price of unbranded ibuprofen. Looking at my dwindling supplies I was beginning to regret my miserly decision. I took some paracetamol instead, but alas it had little effect. A couple more hours later, and after 20 miles that day, my feet were complaining quite loudly. I arrived at Yearning Saddle mountain refuge hut, which provided me with shelter from the wind. Sitting in the sun with my bootless feet up was lovely. I debated as to whether I should stop there for the night, but after a dinner of bread, cheese and wine, and succumbing to taking a couple of my remaining ibuprofen, I decided to press on to Windy Gyle. At 600m it did run the risk of being a windy night and it was probably called "Windy" Gyle for a reason. Looking at the forecast, which I hoped would prove accurate, the winds were due to abate later in the evening.

With no functioning headphones and no one to disturb I played music through my phone's tiny tinny speaker. It was enough to distract me and gee me on. In fact I found that the combination of red wine, ibuprofen and music was my walking equivalent to a car's engine being injected with nitrous oxide. The next five miles flew by in a blur. Fortunately Windy Gyle wasn't too windy and I pitched without a problem. Only 12 miles to go to Kirk Yetholm, which was to have been the end point but now marked only half way.

Swift walking on cinder logging lorry tracks.

Churned up paving stones on The Cheviots.

DAY 14

Windy Gyle to Kirk Yetholm to Auchope Mountain Hut
Weather: Clear, sunny day and hot afternoon
23.5 miles
3300ft ascent

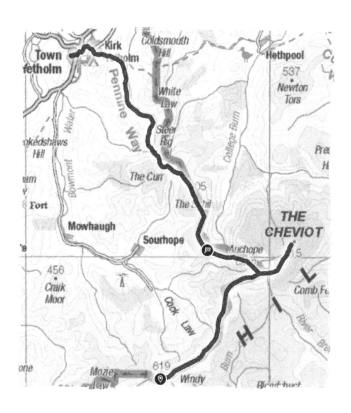

Once again I was wide awake well before 5am. It had been a frosty night and continued to be a chilly morning. My milk carton contained icy lumps. Warming tea and Readybrek prepared me for the day. Looking at the map I discovered I had three bonus Pennine Way miles to walk to tag the Cheviot, the namesake of the Cheviot Hills, and at 777m it marked the highest point. I was getting low on water, but decided that if I was going to summit the Cheviot, it was now or never. I started the day without ibuprofen and wondered how far I would get.

The summit was a tad underwhelming, being mostly flat peat bog not unlike the top of Kinder where I'd started the walk almost two weeks ago. There was a small wooden cross planted in earth, perhaps a memorial to someone who had died. It had the inscription, "The impossible is nothing" upon it. In that moment, having walked 250 miles, I gave it a nod of agreement.

I did bump into another walker, who kindly gave me half a litre of water. The water was most needed as I still had another three hours of plodding up and down and the day was warming up. At the Schil I was beginning to feel thirsty so opted to take the low route down to Kirk Yetholm. This linked up with a burn within an hour and I was able to brew up several much-needed teas.

Arriving in Kirk Yetholm was a bit of an anticlimax. I'm not sure what I had expected. Marching bands? Ticker tape parades? Fireworks? None of those things occurred. In fact the Borders Inn, the official end of the Pennine Way and where you allegedly receive a free drink on completion of the walk, was closed. I later found out that Scotland had different Covid restrictions in place and

the pubs couldn't open till the following Monday. I had
arrived on a Friday. It wasn't a huge disappointment as I
hadn't walked the Pennine Way just for a free pint. Besides,
technically, due to Covid rules, I wasn't supposed to be in
Scotland anyway. I counted my blessings that I hadn't been
arrested by roving border guards.

What Kirk Yetholm lacked in pubs, it made up for with
public water taps. I drank plentifully and rehydrated. In
Town Yetholm, half a mile further, I also discovered that
the community shop was not only open but thriving. To
paraphrase Mark Twain, "Internet reports of its demise
were greatly exaggerated." I bought a bumper pack of
Crunchies, wine, a delicious slice of homemade quiche and
a coronation chicken sandwich. I hadn't eaten a coronation
chicken sandwich probably since, well, the coronation. The
community shop also stocked ibuprofen, the affordable
non-branded stuff at that, although by that point I would
have paid anything for the drug. I snaffled my booty,
making use of yet another conveniently placed picnic table
on the village green, and messaged my family and friends.

I barely stayed an hour before I turned around and
retraced my steps back into the hills. The afternoon was
silly hot for Scotland in April. I had filled my jumble of
water bottles at the village taps on my way out – a total of
two and a half litres. Despite the weight, remembering my
thirst from the morning and the lack of water available on
the tops, I wished I could carry more.

With the water, supplies from the shop, and my coat
and fleece stowed, my pack was about as heavy as it
got. I had read somewhere that you risked injury if you
carried more than 20% of your body weight. My weight

is somewhere around 75kg, from which I calculated my maximum pack weight should be 15kg at the upper end. In my favour I had been walking for two weeks so was relatively fit. My pack didn't feel impossibly heavy, but it was a very warm afternoon.

I walked slowly, taking advantage of the proximity of the route to Halter Burn to regularly fill my sun hat with water and pour it over my head. Despite the cooling measures, it was a very warm three hours before I came to the Auchope mountain refuge hut. This was a different hut to the one where I had stopped for dinner the day before. The Cheviots are well endowed with refuge shelters, which hinted at the need for them due to inclement weather. I couldn't believe my good luck at crossing the Cheviots on what was probably statistically the only two consecutive days of good weather each year.

Mountain refuge huts are fine places to escape hypothermia in atrocious weather but are absolutely not the greatest places to sleep if the sun is shining and the wind isn't trying to blow you off the hill. I pitched my tent on a level grassy patch just behind the hut and enjoyed peanuts, a Crunchie bar and wine from my lofty position as the sun set. I was in a thoughtful mood as I pondered that the walks I do are rarely about reaching the end. The end just marks a new beginning.

I called my family and they passed on their congratulations. I also felt that they missed me, each in their own ways with their own needs. I struggled to explain to myself, let alone them, why I felt the need and had the compulsion to walk back again. Surely walking 250 miles was enough? I think it was something to do with feeling that I had had too easy a ride. The journey hadn't exactly been effortless but it had been straightforward. Instead of celebrating my good fortune, I felt I hadn't fulfilled my obligation, the unsaid pact that I had made with this long distance walk when I first committed myself to it.

Snow lingering on The Cheviots.

The end of the Pennine Way and my halfway point.

Sublime sunset from Auchope mountain refuge hut.

DAY 15

Auchope Mountain Refuge Hut to Padon Hill
Weather: Clear skies and a warm afternoon
24.5 miles
2200ft ascent

The pressure was now off. I had achieved what I had set out to do. I had walked the Pennine Way. Perversely, the pressure was also now on. I hadn't previously committed myself to this. Now I wanted to push myself. I wanted to see how fast I could complete the Pennine Way. I had nothing to lose. I was awake at 4am. What does it take to get a long, restful sleep? I was away before 7am, keen to make the most of the cool morning. I climbed up to Auchope Cairn in slow motion trying to ease myself into the day gently. I didn't hold back on my replenished supply of ibuprofen as I discovered my third blister of the walk – the result of yesterday afternoon's hot and sweaty schlep up the Schil. After reaching Auchope Cairn the route became more rolling.

I passed an early morning fell runner and was filled with equal amounts of admiration and pity. What an amazing feat! Who would do this to themselves? I registered an inward concern that I might be leaning towards the fell runner's euphoric/masochistic mindset. In the still early hours of the morning I passed another walker. He was burdened with a pack larger than mine and he was probably half my age. I asked if he was walking the Way. He wasn't; he was a local out for the weekend. I took the opportunity to grill him on regional dialect. Having read the name "Kirk Yetholm" so many times, I had always wondered how it was pronounced. In my head I'd been saying "Kirk Yeth-Home". Now I know. If anybody asks you, phonetically it's "Kir-Yeh-umm".

When I passed Windy Gyle summit, I realised that I must have missed the summit proper on my way north and wondered if I'd camped on the right hillock at all as it was so unfamiliar. Clearly there are limitations to turbo charging myself with cheese, chocolate and wine. Reading my map going south now rather than north, I kept getting befuddled, as my brain hadn't caught up with the readjustment of direction and the fact that I was now heading home.

I passed a marauding band of wild Cheviot goats. I sensed I was participating in a surreal reenactment of The Three Billy Goats Gruff story, where I was the troll asking permission of the goats to be allowed to go on my way unharmed. But I had no big brother troll to help me. The hairy feral reprobates allowed me to pass unmolested. I made good progress and stopped for an 11am lunch at Yearning Saddle mountain hut – the hut I had stopped at for dinner with aching feet only two days ago but now that felt like the long-distant past.

As the day warmed up I was conscious of rationing my water. Fortunately I got down and off the Cheviots without feeling too thirsty. I passed the same house where I had acquired water on my way north. The owner was in her garden again, and again I asked for water. She remembered me from before. I was probably reasonably hard to forget. Her daughter obliged my request for water.

I enjoyed the easy, sheltered walking along the River Rede. It was quite a contrast to the exposed lofty Cheviots behind me. I arrived at the picnic bench where I had brewed up a few days ago. It all felt a little déjà vu-ish retracing my steps. This time at 5pm I was feeling tired and I considered stopping for the night. I feasted on curry noodles, cheese, bread and hot chocolate. Looking at distances I reckoned I could make Alston the evening after next with the chance of a pub meal. Feeling revived by dinner and the prospect of a future pub meal, I walked another five miles and camped just short of Padon Hill, where I spied a nice, flat grassy spot not far from the path. After pitching my tent, I had a late-ish supper of peanuts, Snickers bar and Metaxa.

Wild goats on the Cheviots.

Finger post on the Cheviots.

DAY 16

Padon Hill to Hadrian's Wall
Weather: Clear skies, a warm afternoon
21.5 miles
1900ft ascent

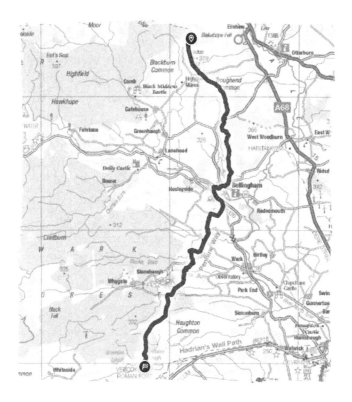

I drifted from blissful sleep and was brought back to full consciousness with a start. I felt pain. Quite a bit of pain. What? Where? When? How? Why? Various bits of body were clamouring for attention. I remembered that I was walking the Pennine Way ... and that I might be pressing myself a bit too hard. After several sips of tea and several chocolate brioche buns for breakfast, I took a couple of ibuprofen. Slowly my body stopped mutinying and the complaints were dialled down.

Outside the tent I was greeted with a grey, cool, overcast morning. I lost the path somewhere between Padon Hill and Hazel Brook beck. Clearly featureless rolling moorland is another of my navigational Achilles heels. Throw in a few tempting quad bike tracks and I was easily lured off the path towards destinations unknown. I counted my lucky stars that I lived in the age of GPS and ViewRanger. I also felt a bit of a fraud for cheating at times on the navigation front.

I arrived in the town of Bellingham (apparently pronounced "Bellin-Gam") late morning. My wife had sent me a package but it hadn't arrived. I had requested headphones, tea bags, toothpaste and toilet paper. Not exactly a deal breaker but it would have been most welcome. Visiting the local chemist I stocked up on Compeed and ibuprofen, more out of insecurity than actual need. I liberated two more excellent pies from the bakery, which I munched on sitting at what I now considered to be "my" bench. I had to queue to shop at the Co-op for my onward supplies. It was a Saturday and Bellingham was quite busy.

Walking south I was struggling to charge my phone

as the solar panel was nowhere near as functional. Even attaching it to my front didn't much improve my phone charging. Looking like a Cyberman did attract the odd look from passersby. I arrived at Horneystead Farm, where I once again made good use of the shower and shaved for the first time in two weeks. I also did some more rudimentary washing of my boxer shorts and socks. Chatting more to Helen, I felt humbled by her and her partner's walking achievements. I reminded myself that whatever I seek to do, there will always be someone who has done it faster, higher and further. The race was only and always against myself.

And just to reiterate this lesson, a couple of hours on I bumped into a bloke doing the Pennine Way. He was the first person I had encountered also following the route. We passed each other in the commercial forests just north of Hadrian's Wall. He didn't look like a typical wayfarer, as he lacked a substantial backpack and the usual walking poles. He told me he'd covered the first 80 miles in just 24 hours. I misheard him and thought he had done the first 18 miles in 24 hours. It wasn't until I had quizzed him three times that I realised the distance he had covered. My mind struggled to comprehend a human, any human, covering 80 miles in 24 hours. He did concede that he had suffered a groin injury with such exertion and that he was being supported by his brother in a camper van, who provided meals and accommodation. Still, he was on his fifth day and on course to finish the Pennine Way the following day. By way of an apology he divulged that he'd only just managed to complete the Bob Graham round. The Bob Graham round is a masochistic endurance task where people run 42 fells in the Lake District in 24 hours. I was not sure if he was taunting me or encouraging me.

I camped just short of Hadrian's Wall, conscious that good weather on a Saturday might result in a few tourists up on the wall. My new-found favourite dinner of the moment was lardons and couscous followed by a Crunchie. Quick, easy and delicious.

Camping just north of Hadrian's Wall.

DAY 17

Hadrian's Wall to the River South Tyne just before Garrigill
Weather: Cold start then sunny
23 miles
1850ft ascent

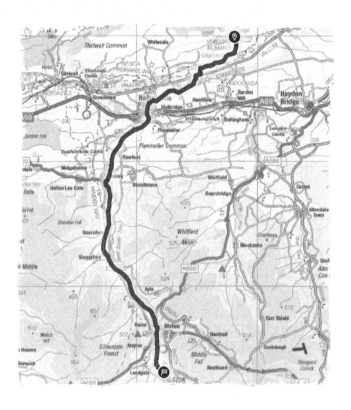

I woke up at 3.30am in pain again, but this time it was just my latest blister, blister number four, screaming at me. I soothed it with ibuprofen and went back to sleep. It was a frosty start and I read on the BBC website what I already suspected – it was officially the driest and frostiest April on record.

My first obstacle of the day appeared in the form of a large field with a dozen or more cows with their young calves. As I climbed the stile, all heads turned to eye me. I could see that the path went diagonally across the field, connecting with a line of flagstones across a boggy river that ran through the middle. I opted to hug the perimeter. I decided that a pair of soggy feet was a fair trade for not getting mauled by protective cows.

Arriving at Hadrian's Wall I avoided the Pennine Way, as it followed the wall closely, with many steep ups and downs. I walked a couple of hundred metres to the south where the path was more undulating and then deserted the Way entirely and cut into Haltwhistle to pick up sandwiches for lunch. Haltwhistle turned out to be a charming town with friendly natives on the sunny morning that I visited. Although the day started crisp, it soon warmed up. Passing a local chap weeding his garden, I asked for water and he kindly complied, taking my water bottles. When he returned from his house with the bottles, he also brought me a full glass of water, which I gratefully slurped down. At the Sainsbury's I caused minor havoc, bumping into displays with my pack. The staff were understanding and I bought not only sandwiches for lunch but a new pair of earbuds. Given the choice between a cheap £8 pair and Sony ones for £15, I went crazy and splurged on the Sony earbuds.

Studying the route on my phone I hatched a cunning plan that would see me in Alston late afternoon/early evening with the chance of a proper meal. Once again I spurned the Pennine Way in favour of the River Tyne Trail. This promised a direct straightforward 15-mile walk to Alston and just the same views as the Pennine Way. A mile after leaving Haltwhistle I even found a sunny bench to eat my sandwiches on. I put my newly purchased earbuds to good use and five hours of plodding disappeared in a blur. I briefly paused to admire the views from the top of Lambley viaduct and realised that it was a perfect viewing platform above where I had washed in the river below a week earlier on my way north. I shuddered at the thought of how many tourists I might have traumatised by the sight of me brandishing my naked flesh.

Coming into Alston I met another wayfarer, Lee. Heavy pack, check. Walking poles, check. He was a cheery fellow, who had done no research, bought a guidebook at the last minute in Edale and wasn't even checking the weather. Part of me admired his blasé approach to the Pennine Way; however, the more sensible side of me knew that such a laissez-faire attitude could end in disaster. I had learned the hard way on a previous walk, almost freezing blundering through blizzards. Still, his luck was holding out and I wished Lee well with the rest of the walk.

My first port of call in Alston was the Spar where I had purchased the substandard earbuds six days earlier. I hadn't kept the receipt but the manager kindly took me at my word. She exchanged the shoddy old pair which I had held onto due to my disgust at their appalling durability. As it happens the new pair stayed unopened in their packaging at the bottom of my pack for the rest of the walk. My Sony earbuds continued to work brilliantly.

Next stop was The Turks Head pub, which was open but not doing food, so I headed into the Co-op next door. I bought a good selection of treats as I reasoned that I was going to eat most of it before I left town. Packing my hoard away I spotted an open fast food burger cafe across the square. Ignoring that I'd just purchased enough food to feed me for two days (never shop for food when you've walked 20 miles and are hungry!) I ordered a burger and chips. Waiting for my order to arrive I snaffled a Co-op Simply Irresistible prawn cocktail starter, a selection of cured Italian meats and a tub of olives. There aren't many perks of walking 10 hours a day, day after day, but eating as much as you want is definitely one of them. I took my burger, chips and a bottle of Merlot and found a quiet park bench tucked away in a corner of Alston. I'm not sure what the passersby made of me stuffing myself with chips and drinking wine from a large plastic camping mug but I was far beyond caring about my self-image at that point.

Suitably sated and feeling a little merry I rejoined the Pennine Way and headed out of town before I could be arrested for my hobo tendencies. I followed the River South Tyne and camped not far from where I had pitched on the way north a week earlier, just north of Garrigill. Recalling that the next part of the Way was on dull 4x4 track to Greg's Hut, then a circuitous route over Cross Fell and down to Dufton before returning on track at High Cup Nick, I fired up ViewRanger to see if there was an alternative. Studying the map, I plotted another cunning plan. I worked out a route which was more direct, probably saving five miles, and was also through wilder territory.

Lambley viaduct.

DAY 18

Garrigill to River Tees just before Middleton-in-Teesdale
Weather: Partly cloudy, coolish
23 miles
1850ft ascent

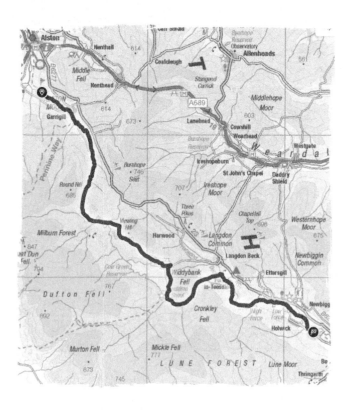

I enjoyed a relatively warm night that was practically tropical compared to the glacial mornings I had become used to. I didn't even need to scrape ice off the tent. Chocolate chip brioche buns had become my new stand-in in lieu of Readybrek for breakfast. I reviewed my cunning plan to check it was viable in the bright light of day. It still looked doable. It involved following the River Tyne Trail south to the source of the River Tyne then a couple of miles of trackless bog hopping east where I would hopefully link up with a path that would take me to Cow Green Reservoir and I'd rejoin the Pennine Way at Cauldron Snout. Simple. It did mean that I'd miss out High Cup Nick, but I felt it was a worthwhile trade-off for the pointless dogleg to Dufton. Besides, having camped there on the way up and enjoyed a lovely sunset and sunrise, I thought I'd done it justice.

As a precaution I did send my wife a message outlining my new plan, with instructions to forward the details to Mountain Rescue if she hadn't heard from me in 24 hours. Trackless bog hopping isn't always easy and footpaths marked on maps aren't always there in the real world. Under yet another clear sky I followed the River Tyne Trail past Garrigill, initially through farmland generously sprinkled with lambs and their mums. Evidence of civilisation became sparser and meadows dropped away to ever more wilder moorland. Where the Tyne becomes a fledgling burbling trickle, I found its source is marked by a large stone sculpture. I found it thought-provoking that even a river as mighty as the River Tyne has humble beginnings.

I could just about see the golf ball radar off on a hilltop in the distance. With fells all round I felt as

embedded in the wilderness as I ever had been since
setting off from Edale weeks ago. I walked another mile
south along a track, then took a bearing east, making
good use of a gamekeeper's quad trail part of the way,
before I started through trackless moorland. With the
beautiful sunny day and dry conditions underfoot it was
all completely non-threatening. Something of a non-event.
Relaxing too much I did almost come unstuck. Letting
my guard down crossing a river I was getting cocky and
lost my footing. I stumbled and just caught myself before
a rocky fall. It could have been nasty. I was in the middle
of nowhere with no phone signal. That would not have
been a great place to break a leg. I scolded myself for my
complacency. Within half an hour I breathed a sigh of
relief as I connected with the path marked on the map,
which turned out to be quite a substantial gravel track.
A veritable highway across the fells. After a few more
uneventful miles I arrived at Cow Green Reservoir, which
even boasted mobile phone reception. I messaged my wife
advising that she could stand down the Mountain Rescue. I
didn't mention my near miss.

Down by Cauldron Snout I was surprised at the
progress I was making. Even the rocky section along
the River Tees wasn't too daunting or as arduous as I
remembered. Maybe it was my familiarity? I stopped for
a hot chocolate break and bumped into Jack, another
wayfarer. He was a lovely bloke from Mirfield in West
Yorkshire, which wasn't far from where I lived, although
he was now based in London. I discovered that he worked
as an orthotist, making custom shoes for people. Ironically,
considering his expertise in feet, he had neglected his own
feet and was suffering from many blisters. He was hoping

to meet up with his dad at Hadrian's Wall to complete the walk together. I gave him a handful of Compeed blister plasters and wished him luck.

Revived with hot chocolate I plugged myself into some tunes. Time and distance seemed to fly by along the River Tees. I enjoyed Teesdale much more than the first time round. The absence of grockles and the overcast sky made the place much more atmospheric. I stopped for the night a couple of miles north of Middleton-in-Teesdale. I was passing through farmland with many sheep and lambs. I had seen a few signs stating, "No Camping", which put me on my guard. I knew it was illegal to wild camp anywhere in England, but when there are signs about it, it means locals are probably on the lookout. Although I have never experienced any problems myself, I have heard the odd third party story of farmers stamping on tents. I found what I hoped would be an out-of-the-way spot in a corner of a field. It even had a stream running into the River Tees. Perfect for sourcing water. I ate my dinner sitting on a stile, getting a feel for the place before I pitched my tent. A farmer did pass through the far end of the field on a quad bike doing his evening rounds checking the sheep, but if he did see me he didn't seem unduly concerned.

I pitched my tent and hoped for the best. My feet were holding up really well considering the mileage covered. Only two lots of ibuprofen were needed. I noted that the epic stretch of good weather was due to break, with showers and strong winds set for the next few days.

The source of the River Tyne.

Trackless bog hopping territory.

DAY 19

River Tees just before Middleton-in-Teesdale to Swaledale
Weather: Cloudy, windy, showery
23.5 miles
2450ft ascent

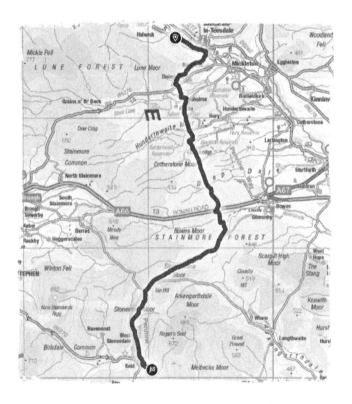

When I woke up, my legs and feet were not screaming at me. In fact, they were not even mildly grumbling. This forfeited the need for morning painkillers. I noted it was the first time in a week that my breakfast didn't include ibuprofen. Contrary to the forecast, I was greeted with a dry start. "Perhaps the rain is yet to come," I thought. I got all of four drops of rain on the tent as I packed up. I hoped my luck would last. It was a pleasant stroll along the river into Middleton-in-Teesdale. There was heavy cloud about, but the sun shone through on occasions. There was a patch of blue sky, just big enough to make a sailor a pair of trousers, as my gran would have said.

I arrived in town at 7.50am, ten minutes before the Co-op opened, so I lurked outside. When the doors did open, I found that they hadn't had their morning restocking deliveries. The shelves were sparse. There was not much choice. I settle for paté and wholemeal rolls for breakfast. Not my usual choice but my body continued to crave calories. I had taken to reading the food labels closely, analysing daily intakes and total energy values. Paté is a great source of calories, as is peanuts. I had worked out that whilst the recommended serving of a 270-gramme packet of Co-op dry roasted peanuts only provides five percent of your recommended daily calorie intake, if I snaffled half the packet in one go, my calorie intake suddenly soared. Not good for weight loss, but for walking 25 miles a day, repeatedly, it's just what I needed. Another well-placed picnic table allowed me to eat breakfast in comfort and restock my pack.

I messaged a friend, "Hopefully the weather isn't too bad. Hopefully the Tan Hill Inn is open. Hopefully it's not raining when I get there. Hopefully it's not too windy in Keld." I realised that the day ahead was based on hope and as the aphorism goes, "Hopefully doth butter no parsnips."

All packed up, I moseyed out of town across a bridge and walked half a mile in the wrong direction. I knew I had gone wrong but struggled to figure out where. The map tiles I used for navigating when travelling north had either been binned or turned into notepaper as I hadn't anticipated walking home until day 10 of the walk near Alston. I was now navigating by memory and ViewRanger. My memory was patchy. I had failed to memorise every step of the 250-mile route. I switched on my phone to consult ViewRanger. Worryingly, a default system menu appeared on my phone with the options of rebooting or wiping all data and a factory reset. A factory reset struck me as a tad severe. I did not want to lose all my photos. I did not want to lose my downloaded Spotify playlists. And most importantly, at that moment, I did not want to lose my ViewRanger maps. Once again I realised how dependent I was on my phone. With a gulp I select the reboot option. Three reboots and eight minutes later, my phone restarted as it should, with everything intact. I drew a deep sigh of relief and retraced my steps to locate a well-hidden truculent Pennine Way finger post.

Back over Harter Fell things seemed to look more familiar and I came across the gamekeeper's house where I'd had a warm welcome on my way north. This time there was no one home. I felt at ease filling my bottles from the exterior tap I had used before. I pushed onwards and passed the reservoirs, noting the second pair of reservoirs where I had camped before.

I wasn't looking forward to the next stretch – the moor where I had struggled to maintain the path and gained my first blister. This time I was much more mindful to keep to the path. I carefully spotted signs to stay on track with minimal detouring. The route to the A66 passed swiftly in under an hour and a half. I questioned how I had found it so challenging travelling north. Sometimes it's a head game. For old times' sake I did get another blister almost exactly where I had gained my first blister of the walk, both geographically and anatomically. It turned out to be the last blister of the walk.

I met another wayfarer – a rather dour French/ Scottish chap. French by parentage but Scottish by upbringing, which perhaps explained his lack of humour and sullenness. He was now living in Milton Keynes, which may or may not have added to his stern outlook. Like all the wayfarers I had stumbled upon, he had had a tough lockdown and walking the Pennine Way was his way of reconnecting with the great outdoors.

Only half an hour later, just after crossing the busy A66, I met an entirely different wayfarer – a much more jolly chap from Sheffield. He had just walked through a substantial shower and was shrugging it off, like water off a duck's back. Admittedly, he had had an easier recent journey, having stayed at the Gargrave Holiday Inn and then glamped in a yurt in Keld. I admitted to the odd pang of envy. He was carrying a few more years than me, but his partner was keeping him on track and supporting him along the way. I briefed him on a few good wild camping sites ahead and we wished each other luck.

Crossing Sleightholme Moor the sky was heavy, dark

and threatening. Cloud bursts exploded all around me – to the east, the west, the south and behind me to the north. I guessed it was only a matter of time before I received a soaking, so it was with some amazement that I arrived at the Tan Hill Inn in a fairly dry state. There were only a few punters at the UK's highest pub – not surprising, considering the weather and the fact that at this point in Covid pandemic times, pubs were restricted to only serving outside. I continued to count my good fortune at arriving ten minutes before the pub's kitchen closed for an hour for evening food preparation. I cannot fault the Tan Hill Inn. They had erected sails and installed gas heaters to make al fresco dining about as palatable as it could get for the UK in April. Due to the inclement weather, my solar panel had been rendered useless, so my phone battery was dwindling. Upon request, though, they provided a phone charger whilst I feasted on lamb shank, my favourite all-time meal, and guzzled a bottle of Merlot then splurged on sticky toffee pudding. Not a cheap meal, but considering how few meals out I had eaten and the amazing hospitality, I considered it a bargain.

The rain caught up with me as I sheltered under the Tan Hill Inn's sails. The sails struggled to hold at bay the worst of the Yorkshire weather. Staff obligingly periodically popped over to push off and empty the reservoir of water that built up in the overhead canvas. I chatted to the chap who had been serving me and paid respect to his hardiness and the inn's preparation for Covid times. He told me he was in his element being outside in a t-shirt regardless of the weather and that the entire outside area had been prepped by their caretaker/handyman using basic wood whilst conforming to the council's temporary building development rules. He reckoned that the outside area was so popular that they would maintain the outdoor dining situation even after Covid rules eased. I paid my bill and wished them well.

On leaving I passed a couple of new arrivals, who were now to be the only customers at the inn. With big packs and walking poles they were clearly wayfarers. I stopped to say hello on my way out. They appeared disheartened and I tried to lighten their spirits. I wasn't sure if I had done a good job, but wished them well on their Pennine Way quest. I had what I hoped was a sheltered evening destination in mind, where I had camped on the way up. It was still some miles away, but fuelled by lamb shank and wine nothing was beyond my scope.

Turning on my now charged phone, I picked up a message from my wife. "Call me!!" It sounded urgent. I became anxious and wondered what had happened. "Are the kids OK?" "Has someone died?" I phoned her straight away, slightly panicked, to discover the internet was down. I breathed a sigh of relief and exhaled a breath of annoyance. As my wife isn't a named person on the account, our service provider, Plusnet, cannot deal with her. I could feel her frustration. After being disconnected from the world for several weeks, my personal perspective was different. I was at the highest pub in the UK on a bleak, blustery evening with patchy phone reception. I spent a cold half hour on the edge of the car park, the only place with mobile reception, talking to a Plusnet customer services adviser. I must add that it was quite possibly the best customer service that I had ever experienced, both from the Tan Hill Inn bar staff and

Plusnet customer services. In that wintry corner of the world it took me a few attempts to remember my security access information. Once through security I was able to set up my wife as an account holder and organised an OpenReach engineer to go round in the morning.

I was reprieved. Calamity had been averted. The sky had not fallen; however, there was still considerable rain falling from the sky. It was later than I hoped by the time I left the Tan Hill Inn. Next stop was the Keld valley and what I hoped was a sheltered spot from the strengthening winds. I knew where I was headed as it was where I had camped on the way up.

The wind was persistent and troubling in strength. An hour or so later I arrived at my Keld valley location. The first thing I saw was my recalcitrant charger cable lying on the ground exactly where I had dropped it over a week earlier, eying me accusingly for my willful and wanton neglect. I noted but ignored that there were also many twigs strewn across the ground. With no Plan B and the light fading I pitched my tent and hoped for the best.

Ominous sky towards the Tan Hill Inn.

Charger cable and twigs.

DAY 20

Swaledale to Hawes
Weather: Cloudy, windy, wintry showers of sleet
12.5 miles
1950ft ascent

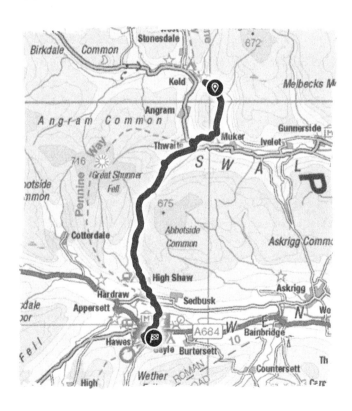

I endured a very windy broken night's sleep. It transpired that my chosen campsite was something of a wind tunnel. That explained the quantity of tree debris strewn across the ground which I had chosen to overlook the night before. My lightweight wonder of a tent survived the battering intact.

Approaching Thwaite it was sleeting heavily and the wind was brisk. My least favourite walking weather. By 9am I was both wet and cold, and that was in the shelter of the valley. Ahead of me Great Shunner Fell was covered in thick, dark, menacing cloud. This was not forecast. Wind is one thing, but persistent sleet, snow and zero visibility high up on a hill is an entirely different kettle of fish. I wished that I could find a nice warm cosy cafe to escape the elements, but Covid rules did not allow indoor eating or drinking. All cafes in Thwaite were firmly closed. I settled for the only shelter I could find – an open-sided lean-to containing an assortment of rubbish bins on a resident's driveway. Sitting on the recycling box with icy wetness lashing down, I made a ham sandwich, stuffing all six slices of ham in the packet into my last bread roll.

I considered my situation. If I was cold in the sheltered valley, I would be freezing up on the hill. I no longer had paper maps for Great Shunner Fell as I had discarded them on my way north before the thought of walking back south had ever entered my mind. Navigating by phone in the rain and snow, trying to use wet frozen fingers on a touchscreen is far from optimal. I reasoned that if I headed up over the hills in these conditions I could well end up becoming a Mountain Rescue statistic. However, staying put wasn't really an option either, as there was nowhere to hide from the atrocious weather in Thwaite. I launched ViewRanger, psyching myself up for action and wondering if I could memorise the next seven miles. Studying the screen I noticed that a road connected Thwaite to Hawes. Whilst I hadn't signed up to the Pennine Way to walk the route on tarmac, I also hadn't signed up to freezing on a hill top. The road offered a solution to my dismal predicament. If I removed the prospect of getting lost, I knew I could cope with seven miles of grim weather. Not getting any warmer, perched on the recycling box, I quickly made up my mind.

I set myself a stiff pace to warm up as the bitter showers continued. The miles passed swiftly enough. I kept an eye on Great Shunner Fell as I walked. The top half of its slopes remained cloaked in a black, angry cloud. Dropping down from Buttertubs Pass, approaching Simonstone, I came across a red telephone box. I didn't think they existed any more except as antiques. The stiff door put up resistance, finally opening with a persistent heave on my part. It was an unconventional, but welcome, escape from the weather. Retrieving my stove from my backpack I set about brewing a much-needed hot chocolate. There was a sign on the wall stating that the telephone box was due to be decommissioned and that I should get in touch if I relied on it. I'm not sure British Telecom had the way I was using the telephone box in mind, but I would be sorry to see it go. Revived by the warm drink and a Crunchie, I set off for Hawes, now only a couple of miles away.

The dour French/Scottish wayfarer I had passed on Cotherstone Moor had told me he'd stayed at a campsite just south of Hawes. Although technically closed to camping due to Covid rules, they were making an exception for wayfarers. Even though I had only been walking for half a day, I decided to stop early for a bit of rest and relaxation and avail myself of Hawes' abundance of eateries in the evening. Arriving at Blackburn Farm, a jolly farmer welcomed me cheerfully. I was the only camper and had the camping field and compact sanitary block all to myself. After pitching my tent in the shelter of a drystone wall, I had a shower to warm up. Snuggling into my sleeping bag to write a few notes at 2pm I found my eyes growing heavy. I lay down and before I knew it I had drifted off fast asleep. My disturbed previous night and the testing morning had caught up with me. I was clearly in need of a siesta. I awoke late afternoon feeling much revived, both mentally and physically. The weather had cleared up whilst I had slumbered. I could now see the tops of the hills, which had a generous dusting of snow. I was so glad I hadn't taken the high route.

Without my backpack on my back I practically floated the mile back into town. I ordered a family-size meat feast pizza from a takeaway. I ate half of the pizza washed down with a bottle of Merlot on yet another convenient park bench. I returned to the campsite and caught up with my wife and the girls on a WhatsApp video call. By dusk I was tucked up in my bed fast asleep.

Thwaite in the foreground and Great Shunner Fell
shrouded in cloud behind.

Telephone box pit stop.

DAY 21

Hawes to Water Houses
Weather: Windy and hail showers
21 miles
3450ft ascent

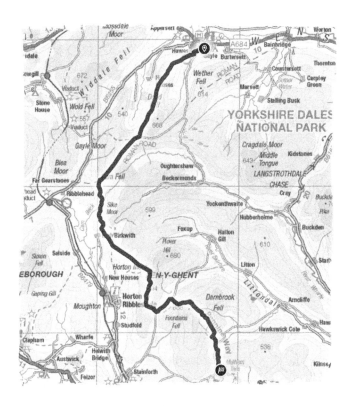

After enjoying a good night's slumber and a lazy morning, I started walking at 8am. I was in a much more positive head space due to the restorative power of sleep. The forecast was for showers, but the day started dry, with the sun shining between clouds. I was much less concerned about being on the tops, as I knew the path finding was straightforward. Fuelled on half a cold meat feast pizza, I felt ready for whatever the day could throw at me. The odd snowflake floated past me on my way up Dodd Fell. I plugged myself into some music and strode on. I was swiftly over the top of the first of the three hills I would cover that day. On the long slope down the other side of Dodd I got hit by the odd squall of hail. The wind was on my back and the hailstones just bounced off my Gore-Tex shell, leaving me dry and warm. I stopped at Lyn Gill for a hot chocolate and peanut snack, but was soon forced on by another shower of hail.

Crossing the Ribble valley heading towards Pen-y-ghent, clouds were once again exploding all around me. Whernside disappeared from view, devoured by a giant cloudburst. I was in sunshine much of the time, feeling lucky that the weather hadn't seriously hit me. It was totally a game of chance. On Pen-y-ghent I saw the heavens open above Fountain Fell. I paused to brew up a hot chocolate in glorious sunshine and watch the action. I shared the summit shelter with a couple. As I took my stove from my backpack the chap quipped, "I bet you've got a tent in there too!" I confirmed that yes I did indeed have a tent and that I had been sleeping in it for the past three weeks. They observed that I must like my own company and I agreed, although I hadn't given it much thought till that moment, and yes, I was quite content with my own solitude and I hadn't felt lonely at all.

We got talking and I discovered that they were relatively new to walking and the great outdoors. They, like many others, had found walking a source of great solace whilst living through various Covid lockdowns. They had covered many of their local footpaths and were branching out. It was the first time they had been up Pen-y-ghent, or any significant hill for that matter. I cautioned them about where it might lead and that before long they might find themselves walking the Pennine Way. They laughed at such an outrageous suggestion. "Stranger things have happened," I warned them.

An hour and a half later, on Fountain Fell, I was in sunshine whilst Pen-y-ghent got dumped on. Despite the weather the views between the dramatic cloudscape were stunningly clear. I could make out the wind turbines in Morecambe Bay and the southern fells of the Lake District on the western horizon.

Coming down off Fountain Fell, the sky grew ominously dark; however, my luck continued to hold and I suffered no more than a few splattering drops of rain. Arriving at the same spot that I had camped at before on my way north, near Water Houses above Malham Tarn, I got the tent up and snuggled in, just as a shower passed through. After a delicious dinner of chorizo, Cheddar, houmous, bread, Crunchie and wine, I pondered where to meet my wife and the girls. My initial idea had been to try and get as far south as possible. To finish the Pennine Way. It was Thursday and I reckoned I could be in Edale by Sunday, but the girls were hoping to rendezvous with me on Saturday afternoon. Add into the mix a fading phone battery and patchy signal and I felt that meeting up could easily get overly complicated for the sake of me trying to finish the return leg. I decided to sleep on it.

Ribblehead viaduct and Whernside.

DAY 22

Water Houses to Helwith Bridge
Weather: Windy and cloudy with the odd shower
14 miles
1600ft ascent

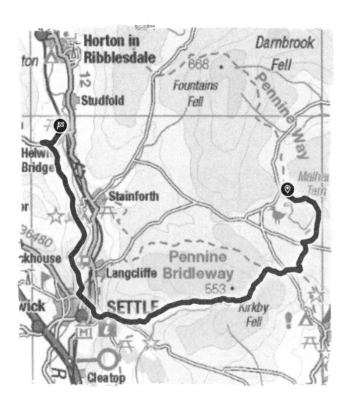

Looking at the map in the morning, I reasoned that after Malham Cove the Pennine Way did get decidedly dull. What's the point of walking south just for the sake of walking, I thought. I did admit to myself that I had just spent three weeks walking for the sake of walking, so perhaps that argument was a little thin. My phone battery charge and phone signal strength were real potential issues, and after being away for so long I did not want to create unnecessary problems for my family. Studying ViewRanger on my phone I noted that Settle was southwest of Malham Cove, with its lure of cafes and not one, but two, Co-ops. I also noted that Helwith Bridge was a few more miles north of Settle along the River Ribble. From previous exploits in this neck of the woods I knew that Helwith Bridge had very little to boast of except for a bridge, obviously, and a very fine inn offering well-priced generously portioned hearty fare. And they allowed casual camping, which was more than enough to seal the deal.

And so, at the top of Malham Cove, I parted with the Pennine Way. I felt I had nothing left to prove. I felt the pact I had made between myself and the Pennine Way had been fulfilled. I had acquired blisters. I had swallowed many painkillers. I had eaten more Cheddar, peanuts, houmous and chocolate than I ever thought humanly possible. I had witnessed more sunrises and sunsets than I had in the past year. I had got lost. I had found my way again. I had been rained on, sleeted on, hailed on and snowed on. My nose was crisp and peeling from too much sun. I had been too cold, too hot and just right. I had chased rainbows. It had been an epic journey. An amazing experience. Thank you and goodbye.

After 400 miles I turned my back on the Pennine Way and redirected myself along the Dales Way to Settle. I felt a weight lifted from my shoulders. I walked for the first time in a while with a lightness that had nothing to do with the weight of my pack. The sense of freedom was liberating. I had made good on the personal pact I had made with the Pennine Way; I had made it to "Kir-Yeh-umm" and walked most of the way back. I had done enough to quell my walking/adventuring and my passion/obsession... for now... until next time.

EPILOGUE

Arriving in Settle, I ordered a Full Yorkshire Breakfast – my first fry-up of the walk. The weather was showery, but after three weeks wandering in the semi-wilderness I was well prepared for al fresco dining. Once my stomach was happy, I bought a few small gifts for the girls. That had become a tradition and a way to say "Thank You" for allowing me the time away on my various nefarious long distance walks. The gifts included handmade mini sheep made with real sheep fleece and pipe cleaners, mini bobble hats from a charity shop knitted by locals (all proceeds to a local charity), a mini felted elephant and mini felted bumble bee, again made locally and a Crunchie bar for each of the girls, made by Mr Cadbury, not local. If you are wondering why my gifts were all "mini" in size, it is because I still had to carry them to the Helwith Bridge Inn several miles away. Once an obsessive lightweight backpacker, always an obsessive lightweight backpacker!

I sauntered the five remaining miles north along the River Ribble stopping, for old times' sake, for a hot chocolate at Stainforth Falls. I arrived at the Helwith Bridge Inn and was met by Paul, the landlord. He claimed that he recognised me. I have visited a number of times, but it had been at least two years since I was last there. He also said it was no problem to camp for the night and that the fee was a whopping three quid. I had a burger and chips for dinner. The following day I did a quick sub-backpack circuit of Pen-y-ghent before my family arrived. We then all celebrated with more burgers and chips. On the Saturday I dragged all the family up Pen-y-ghent. The fourth time for me in two weeks. It is my favourite hill in the Yorkshire Dales. This was followed by more pub grub, and then we escaped before the rain arrived on the bank holiday Monday.

THOUGHTS & REFLECTIONS

The Pennine Way generally runs south to north/north to south as the crow flies. But the actual route contains a few wiggles, some of them substantial, so unless the bird in question is navigationally challenged and had a tipple or two too many, it is far from a straight line. I was happy enough to detour where I felt the Way deviated needlessly, especially on the way back. So to the purest, technically, I haven't walked the Pennine Way, either there or back. I am comfortable with any perceived compromises I made. If my compromises trouble you, this account is not for you.

I love walking in April and May. Spring was definitely ber-doing-ing (the sound that Spring makes?)! Lambs everywhere – bleating, gambolling and tails wagging. Lapwings strutting and fluttering. Rabbits were doing what they are best known for doing. And the weather is at its most dramatic and varied. Snow, rain and sunshine, often in the same day, if not the same hour.

Wild camping is great. It freed me up from any predetermined schedule. However, and best of all, it allowed me to stay deeply embedded in nature amongst some stunning scenery. The only downside is a slightly heavier pack and perhaps being a little more mindful of the weather. I heartily recommend it but always remember the golden rule: respect the environment and leave no trace.

You might think that walking for up to twelve hours a day, day after day, for over three weeks would be the most dull, humdrum, monotonous, stupid, tedious, tame and tiresome thing you could ever do. But I have discovered that time is elastic. The days flew by. Three weeks felt like less than a week. But I also know that looking back, the three weeks I walked the Pennine Way and almost back again will be an eternity branded on my soul. Like the greatest of holidays that passed in a blink of an eye, yet you remember every detail that seems to stretch out forever.

Whilst I had pretty good kit, I know that people were walking the Pennine Way over 50 years before I set off, with much heavier packs. Neanderthals walked far greater distances in nothing more than animal skins. At least some of them survived as we are all living proof of. It's easy to get obsessed with gear, but what really counts is what you carry in your head. An open mind and flexible outlook are more important than the latest Gore-Tex and a GPS.

Compeed and ibuprofen are my friends. I could have gone the purest "my body's a temple" route, but ultimately even temples need upkeep from time to time. I prefer not to suffer undue pain and misery if there are other options.

I did neglect my family. Three weeks away when you have children and a wife is a significant amount of time. Far longer for them than it was for me. I am grateful to them for their understanding. For allowing me to take the time out. For letting me go. For letting me return. I'm pretty sure that they don't understand what drives me. I'm not entirely sure I understand what drives me myself. I do know that I feel so much better for having walked the Pennine Way.

I had forgotten about the physical and mental transformation that occurs when I do a long distance walk. My body craves calories. My body lusts after high-fat foods. Peanuts, Cheddar and houmous become my best friends. I could polish off a tub of houmous in a blink of an eye. A family-size packet of dry roasted peanuts evaporated in a day. I could munch Cheddar without concern. I didn't need high-performance supplements, as natural resources were readily available. By the way, I may have lost a couple of kilos somewhere on the walk, but I'm sure they will find their way back, so I will keep riding a bike between long distance walks to allow me to eat the odd pie.

Initially, I was covering between 15 and 20 miles a day. After a week or so, as I became fitter, my daily mileage naturally increased towards 25 miles. My longest day was 26 miles. I didn't take any rest days, although I did have the odd half day. I'm not very good at sitting still, which I have observed on all my long distance walks. I acquired my first blister on day eight and my fourth and final blister on day nineteen. I'll never know if I would have continued to get blisters if I had kept going, but I suspect if I experienced sweaty or wet days I would. My knees didn't give me any problems during the walk. I do wonder if my ibuprofen consumption during the second half of the walk masked potential problems, as my left knee was a little sore for the week after I had completed the walk and stopped taking ibuprofen. I conclude that I should probably set myself a steadier speed if I want to sustain my pace.

Mentally, it took me a good week to get my head on board with the task at hand. I had had several years to think about the Pennine Way and several months to plan and prepare for it. But it wasn't until I was actually walking it that my head came to terms with the reality. There were moments when I was euphoric, soaring high, experiencing unadulterated elation. Equally, there were moments that I struggled with pain and despair, questioning my motives. I became mindful at some point, somewhere along the return journey, that the walk wasn't about the walk. It was about me walking.

ABOUT THE AUTHOR

Will Cove lives with his long-suffering wife, two daughters and two cats on the northern fringes of the Peak District. When not traipsing around the countryside, he sometimes works as a graphic designer. His passions include travel, paragliding and cooking. He has even been known to combine all three, bundling his family into a small camper van and heading off to explore Europe and a little further afield for a year. Not once but twice.

He generally lives by the mantras of "How hard can it be?" and "What could possibly go wrong?" Even he has to admit, though, that sometimes living by these mantras doesn't work out for the best. When his adages fail him, his unusually well-developed streak of stubbornness to survive has pulled him through the various life-limiting situations he has found himself in. This strategy has always worked for him… so far.

OTHER BOOKS BY WILL COVE

A couple of years before he embarked on the Southern
Upland Way, Will Cove successfully completed his first
ever long distance walk, Wainwright's Coast to Coast.
He just about got from St Bees to Robin Hood's Bay
unscathed. By luck more than judgement. With that single
victory he thought he knew everything there was to know
about walking a long way.

The Southern Upland Way is a coast-to-coast route through southern Scotland, but one which is much less trodden, even by those walkers who have followed in Alfred Wainwright's English coast-to-coast footsteps. There are fewer places to stay. Fewer shops. And most of all, fewer pubs. But where's the adventure if there is no jeopardy? How hard can it be? What could possibly go wrong?

Buoyed by the naive confidence of someone who has no idea of just how much they are lacking in experience, Will gamely bid his family farewell at Portpatrick, on the west coast, and started walking east. Logic suggested the prevailing winds would be on his back, gently helping him each step of the way.

Little did he know that he would spend most of the next two weeks walking into the teeth of the Beast from the East. Through ferocious winds, sideways rain and blizzards. More of an ordeal by ice than a baptism by fire.

This is the account of one fool's stubborn ability to keep going when the conditions strongly suggested he should run away. And how, through adversity, he discovered unexpected shelter, new friendship and hidden treasure.

Whilst this account is by no means a step-by-step guide to walking the Southern Upland Way, if you are toying with the idea of this long distance route, or even if you are just a little curious about what is involved, then you could do worse than learn from the lessons endured by Will and be entertained by his blunders from the comfort of your warm and comfortable living room.

JUST KEEP GOING!

A Cape Wrath Trail Odyssey

Will Cove

The Cape Wrath Trail is the world's finest and toughest long distance walk that no one has ever heard of. Deceivingly, it is more of an idea than a trail, running the length of the Scottish Highlands from Fort William to the most northwestern point of mainland Britain, Cape Wrath. Over 240 miles, passing through magnificent untamed vast empty landscapes. There is no official route and there are no marked trails. Often there is no path at all.

Will Cove first heard of the Cape Wrath Trail whilst hiding from inclement weather in a bothy in the Scottish borders when he walked the Southern Upland Way. Idly lamenting how well the Southern Upland Way was marked and how easy it was to follow, a fellow bothy inhabitant mentioned a mythical walk which lay in the north.

On completing the Southern Upland Way and casting around for another challenge, Will initially dismissed the Cape Wrath Trail as being too long, too tough and too remote. But after several months back home, the seed that had first been sown in the random bothy encounter began to germinate and take root.

So it was, on Good Friday 2019, that Will found himself being waved off by his wife and children on the shores of Loch Linnhe, just across the way from Fort William, and beginning his journey to the most northwesterly point of Scotland, Cape Wrath.

This is the account of one person's walk in to the unknown, both geographically and mentally. A story of the hardship and the beauty of tramping through the Scottish Highlands.

Printed in Great Britain
by Amazon

34129924R00106